The Grace Space

The Grace Space

**The place where the sheer holiness of God
and the depravity of mankind meets and
we are not destroyed**

By Graham Field

Copyright © 2022
All rights reserved.
ISBN: 9798795812380

The Grace Space

DEDICATION

To my Father and Mother, Ernie and Mabel, who raised me in the Christian Faith; to my Father-in-law and Mother-in-law, Abe and Margaret who have encouraged me each step of the way; and to my wife Ann, and children Sharon and David, whom I love dearly.

Grace! 'tis a charming sound,
Harmonious to the ear;
Heaven with the echo shall resound,
And all the earth shall hear.

All sufficient grace!
Never powerless!
It is Christ who lives in me,
In His exhaustlessness.

'Twas grace that wrote my name
In life's eternal book;
'Twas grace that gave me to the Lamb,
Who all my sorrows took.

Grace taught my wandering feet
To tread the pilgrim road;
And new supplies each hour I meet
While pressing on to God.

Grace taught my heart to pray,
And made my eyes o'erflow;
'Tis grace which kept me to this day,
And will not let me go.

Grace all the work shall crown
Through everlasting days;
It lays in love the topmost stone,
And well deserves the praise.

Oh, let that grace inspire
My heart with strength divine;
May all my powers to Thee aspire,
And all my days be Thine. [1]

---

[1] Philip Dodderidge 1715-1751

The Grace Space

Introduction

In 1997 Philip Yancey published, what turned out to be, one of the most informative books on the subject of Grace. '*What's so amazing about Grace.'*

He stated that the word 'Grace' was the last best word in the English Language. I suppose what he meant by that was, a word that has not been contaminated by fashion, hijacked by some fringe movement, or indeed overworked by religious tradition, and left drained of all beauty and transforming power. It was a word that still meant what it meant when the Hebrew writers penned the words, 'chesed or chen,' and when the Greek writers used the word 'charis;' meaning lovingkindness and unmerited favour. Indeed, the word is 'amazing' etymologically, before it becomes amazing in the actions it describes.

I put pen to paper, not to try and supplant Philip Yancey, I could not hold a candle to such an eminent and inspired author, but because, after nearly 25 years the word Grace needs to echo afresh throughout our churches, and indeed our land. If anything, our society has become even more 'ungraceful' than even Yancey imagined. I suppose I am attempting to produce an echo of what has been so eloquently said beforehand, so that the beauty and wonder of Grace penetrates the hearts and minds of another generation.

I am motivated to write, not because of any particular experience, but simply because of a verse of scripture that has 'jumped off the page' and stands before me, pouring out meaning and application, like the oil pots of Elisha. I must therefore record it. I refer to Romans 5:1,2

> *Therefore, having been justified by faith we have peace with God through our Lord Jesus Christ, through whom also we have access by faith into this grace in which we stand, and rejoice in hope of the glory of God.*

Obviously, the phrase which speaks so loudly is, 'The Grace in which we stand.' And hence, 'The Grace Space.'

Graham Field 2022.

The Grace Space

CONTENTS

ACKNOWLEDGMENTS

To my friends and co-workers in the Gospel who have helped in different ways to produce this book, a big thank you from the bottom of my heart.

CHAPTER ONE

Grace; a definition

The crossing of the Red Sea. Exodus 14:14-31.

Throughout this book I hope to show how God, and men and women, under the motivation of the Holy Spirit of God, created a Grace Space wherein God was able to perform His mighty works of redemption. Also, to define what that Grace Space looked like and what it contained.

In this incident, Moses was commanded to stretch out his rod over the waters. It seems that he did this throughout the night. God caused a mighty wind to blow throughout the night and in the morning the waters were stacked up on either side. The descendants of Jacob then crossed over on dry ground. I see the dry ground as the Grace Space. God forced a pathway between the waters, that would shortly destroy the Egyptians, and held them apart for a sufficient length of time until all had crossed over.

And this water symbolises baptism that now saves you also – not the removal of dirt from the body but the pledge of a clear conscience towards God. It saves you by the resurrection of Jesus Christ. 1 Peter 3:21.

Our passage into eternal life, as symbolised through baptism, is such a `*Grace Space.*` Can we pause for a moment, and imagine this scene and what it was that the descendants of Jacob were commanded to do? A wall of water rose up on either side, towering high over their heads, possibly frozen, but nevertheless defying all the laws of nature, with the distant shore just visible through the narrow tract of land that had appeared.

Would you walk through it? Especially when the Angel of the Lord had gone to the back of the queue! Exodus 14:19. There was not a great deal of faith around either. They were filled with fear, understandably, and began to complain against Moses. They said they would rather serve the Egyptians than Moses' God. Exodus 14:11-12.

The Grace Space can be really scary ground. '*Narrow is the gate and difficult is the way that leads to life.*' (Matthew 7:14) But it is the only ground of salvation. It is formed when mighty irreconcilable forces are separated so that redemption can take place. This was not the same as the crossing of the Jordan some 40 years later. Jordan was a flowing river. God only blocked the waters on one side, the other side simply drained away. This was a crossing through the sea and the waters were on both sides.
Grace is a space God made for an undeserving people to experience His mighty power and escape from an unrepentant enemy in order to fulfil His plan for World Redemption.
The Grace Space is that blood-stained pathway that is laid out before us as the only place where our feet are sure, while the wrath of God, the depravity of man, and the raging of Satan

is on every side. Before us is the land of promise and the hope of eternal life.

Etymology.

The word has come to us from the Latin 'gratia' through the Old French to our English form. Its meaning has been constant, *'to show unmerited favour.'* It carries with it the words; favour, mercy, pardon, gratitude, elegance and agreeable.
In Biblical terms it is preceded by the Greek *'Charis'* and the Hebrew *'Chen and Chesed.'*

The Hebrew *'Chen and Chesed'.*

The term first appeared in regard to Noah. It is mostly translated as 'grace or favour' *'Chen'* and describes 'the face' or the attitude Noah perceived God had towards him. It occurs about 70 times in the Old Testament.

The other closely related word is *'Chesed.'* It is translated as lovingkindness, mercy, goodness, steadfast love, and unfailing love.
Together, *'chen and chesed'* define the word Grace in the Old Testament.

The Greek 'Charis'.

The word and its derivatives appear over 100 times in the New Testament. The only other aspect it would introduce is *'gift.'* As such it describes something given by one to another altruistically without any solicitation.

Some quotes on Grace.

'Grace is God's best idea. His decision to ravage a people by love, to rescue passionately, and to restore justly - what rivals it? Of all

his wondrous works, grace, in my estimation, is the magnum opus.'
Max Lucado

'Grace is the voice that calls us to change and then gives us the power to pull it off.' Max Lucado

'We can be certain that God will give us the strength and resources we need to live through any situation in life that he ordains. The will of God will never take us where the grace of God cannot sustain us.' Billy Graham

*'In the New Testament grace means God's love in action towards men who merited the opposite of love. Grace means God moving heaven and earth to save sinners who could not lift a finger to save themselves. '*J. I. Packer

*'Grace is the overflowing favour of God, and you can always count on it being available to draw upon as needed. '*Oswald Chambers

'A man is not saved against his will, but he is made willing by the operation of the Holy Ghost. A mighty grace which he does not wish to resist enters into the man, disarms him, makes a new creature of him, and he is saved. ' Charles Spurgeon

The Doctrine of Grace.

The modern church deals more with subjects, ideas, or teachings, not so much with doctrines. It is the poorer for that in my opinion. The word 'doctrine' has become a little scary in recent years, but we will look and see what it means. A doctrine is an accumulation of ideas and principles assembled from all references on a particular subject from the scriptures.

The broader the reference base the more certain, or dogmatic, is the conclusion. The narrower the reference base, the less certain the conclusion is, and hence the less emphatic the doctrine. As the scriptures tend to present a slightly different emphasis at each reference point the tension created has the effect of whittling down the options, that is, one reference sharpens the meaning of another, so that a concise statement of belief can be made.

It is more than just believing what the bible says. We are all very clear on what the text contains. We can read it in any number of versions and in Latin, Greek and Hebrew. The matter is, as we shall see, always what the text means. It is too simplistic to say '*the bible means what it says.*' While that is true, the cliche does not solve the problem. Groups as diverse as the Jehovah's Witnesses, Presbyterians, Methodists, and Pentecostals, all say they believe what the bible says, yet there is still wide disagreement as to what it means.

The Bible has come to us from the Hebrew, through Greek, Latin, and Old English to modern English without autographs.[2] We need above all, the witness of the Holy Spirit who inspired it in the first place, and some knowledge of who wrote it, to whom, and under what circumstances.
Once a doctrine is established in this way it is presented as part of a creed and all subscribers to that creed are obliged to believe and practice it.

Grace would seem to be one of the easier challenges as the word and words with similar meaning occur hundreds of times in the text.
It is indisputable that Grace is an attribute of the Divine. John 1:14; Romans 1:7, God instinctively provides favour to his people. It is also one of the highest of human virtues, Luke 1: 30, and is noted by God wherever it is found. Grace can be seen as an act of generosity which produces goodness and benefit, whether it be from God to man or from man to man

Grace is the exchange of favour from one who has the

---

[2] Original Manuscripts by the original authors.

capacity to show such favour, but has no obligation to do so, to the one whose only hope is that the favour is bestowed, although he has no right to expect it. [3]

Therefore, Grace is compatible with concepts such as, favour, mercy, forgiveness, repentance, benevolence, blessing, goodwill, kindness and generosity.

It is from the use of these words, either in direct statements or in recounting of narratives that we are able to form the Doctrine of Grace.

Grace covers all acts of Divine favour towards mankind but what is of most significance to us here is Saving Grace, the Grace that deals with the guilt and power of sin and enables a person to be clothed in righteousness.

We know that the supreme purpose of the Scriptures is to reveal to us how God will accomplish the restoring of relationship between mankind and himself. All the complexities involved can be summed up in the one principal word, Grace.

'For it is by Grace you have been saved.' Ephesians 2:8.

The Dilemma.

If only it remained that simple. Although we are all in agreement as to what Grace is, how it is to be imparted has been the subject of controversy throughout the history of Christianity. The bone of contention is the way in which the Sovereignty of God and the autonomy of man can be reconciled. Did God choose me, or did I choose him? In fact, do I actually choose anything regarding my relationship with God, or am I 'pre-programmed' to believe or not believe? It is surprising how ingrained that concept is.

When you try and introduce Christianity to someone and they

---

[3] *Mea Verba*

wish to avoid the subject, you will often get the response, '*Oh I am not religious.*' It is said as if being religious is a result of some special mental or genetic programming which they do not have, so it is pointless raising the subject, they are incapable of responding.

Can Grace, once obtained, be forfeited, or is one's status secure come what may? Does it matter? I believe it does because it fundamentally affects how we present the gospel and how people respond.

Grace is inseparably linked to the other biblical concepts of foreknowledge, election, and predestination.

Grace is the magnificent gift of God, capable of transforming the sinner into a saint. If it is so powerful and is offered freely to all, why are not all saved? Is the power of the human will to refuse Grace, greater than Grace itself? Is not God's will therefore regulated by human will, as God is not willing for any to perish, but they do?

Is not Grace therefore a weaker force than human depravity it is trying to reverse? Therefore, is the potency of Grace only possible when it is 100% effective? In which case Grace could only have been extended to those who believed. This would mean that Grace was not placed at the disposal of those who did not believe, rendering their salvation impossible, and proving the '*I am not a religious person,*' right.

Is my will so powerful that I can actually step out from God's Grace? If this is possible, what assurance is there that I will make it in the end? If my will is involved in my salvation does that not detract from the goal of salvation, which is to Glorify God alone? If my salvation is eternally secure, does it matter how I live? And so, the questions roll on and on.

The Timelessness of God

I am mindful that when we come to encounters between the Divine and the human there are unique factors to bear in mind. They include the fact that God is a being that resides in timeless eternity. He knows no past, present or future. All things are at any one time always before him. He is at one and the same time both the Alpha and the Omega, the Beginning and the End. (Revelation 1:8).

The passing of time is one continuous event. He sits above the circle of the earth. (Isaiah 40:22). In other words, as the orbit of the earth causes the elapse of time and creates a yesterday, today, and tomorrow, he is above it. It does not age him or affect him in any way. He was able to reveal himself to Moses as '*The I am.*'

When we read of the steps involved in applying God's Grace, we automatically want to list them in a sequence of events. Yet when God planned these acts from His viewpoint as the eternal, all-seeing God they would appear as concurrent. Grace was a singular, yet all-embracing act of benevolence of God on behalf of man.

What has the Bible text recorded?

The verses listed here are the main passages that are related to the subject of Saving Grace. They explain how God has provided such a thing as Grace and how sinful beings can enter it. Let us briefly survey them to see what they are saying. We will visit these words many times as we observe what different commentators have made of them. We will then set out on a journey to see how they have been woven into human experience.

John 6:44. There is a predilection to grace.

When someone comes to the time where they are inclined to believe the gospel and commit their lives to Christ, that inclination indicates that there has already been a process of Grace in the person's life in some mysterious form. This John describes as the '*drawing of the Father.*'

It is evident that when Paul was converted it was not his first encounter with the Grace of God. It may have been the first time he was aware of it, at least, was the first time he had yielded to it. Previously he had '*kicked against the goads of Grace.*' Goads were devices used primarily to direct cattle along a certain pathway.

They inflicted moderate pain so that the required direction would be taken. We do not know precisely what form they took with Paul but it is clear they were acts of the Grace of God, which although uncomfortable were there to direct him to Christ. Jesus said in John 16:8, that the Holy Spirit will '*convict*' the world of sin. That is to cause a mental discomfort regarding the state in which one lives in order to cause a change of direction.

Let us by way of example imagine a man with a reputation for godless deeds. We see him with tears and agony of the soul at the altar of a church. There are tears of remorse, prayers of confession, and vows of repentance. And then we see that man rising from his knees with a sense of acceptance and forgiveness, stepping out into a new life in Christ.

How much of what we observed was the sovereign act of God, and how much was the decision making of the man? All the forensic evidence would point to the fact that it was the act of the man concerned. However, we would have also been aware of the fact that some prior experience had brought that man to that state, and on enquiry, we would have found that to be an act of God. It is at that point that the activity of redemption becomes a mystery and passes from the scope of finite understanding.

Most, if not all, believers will testify to this aspect of Grace. The preliminary acts will range from the devotion of a believing friend, even the pain of current circumstances, or the prayers of a loving family. The point is, the moment of conversion does not come out of the blue. Grace has already been at work. It implies that something had taken place in the heart of God concerning an individual, before it took place in the heart of the individual.

Acts 2:23. `*The determined purpose and foreknowledge of God'* delivered Jesus to you. The act of Grace in the sending of Jesus, is clearly something God planned, and foresaw its result. This plan put the Son of God into human hands to do as they desired. Then God took over again and raised him from the dead. The events of Calvary were a combination of Divine and human activity. The human activity was totally volitional. The individual people were not programmed to do what they did, even though God had foreseen that they would do what they did. We know they were responsible because they were invited to repent of it. (Acts 2: 38). You cannot repent of what you are not responsible for.

We can see that the outworking of Grace on earth was foreseen in heaven before it came to pass. But it was in the phrase `*lawless hands,'* where the problem lay. They did not crucify Jesus to procure the good that God intended, they took him to silence his testimony and thereby they were guilty. Despite their intention and action, God produced the good he had foreseen.
This directs us to consider that the outworking of Grace on earth has been foreseen by God. We shall return to these thoughts many times in this book as we examine how they have been interpreted differently over the years.

Romans 8:28-33. These verses will also re-occur frequently in this book. From these verses we pick up important words that are inextricably linked to the Grace of God. They are namely; calling, foreknowledge, predestined, conformed, justified, and glorified. Similarly in Ephesians 1:3-6 we find the phrase, *'chosen in him before the foundation of the world.'* In verses 11-12 we have *'predestined'* again. In Ephesians 2:1-2 we have the phrase *'dead in sins,'* reflecting human inability, and in 2:8 the all-important, *'By grace you have been saved through faith and that is not of yourselves but the gift of God.'*

The Elect or Chosen. It seems that in accordance with his sovereignty, God graciously elected or chose a certain number of mankind to benefit from redemption and enter a place of Grace. By default, it would appear to be implied, he designated a certain number who would not benefit.

Foreknowledge. Based on the attribute of omniscience, peculiar to godhood, God knew who would believe and who would not. He saw it before it happened. Whether foreknowledge was passive or active is not initially clarified. In other words, did God act on what he saw, or was it just an observation?

Justified and Glorified. It seems that those whom he elected and foresaw would benefit from redemption, without exception. He graciously provided a pathway to glory which guaranteed that there was enough power in Grace to keep them from falling or failing.

Predestined. He made their destiny sure and irrevocable. What he foresaw he decreed would happen so that whatever circumstances would arise the desired goal would be achieved.

Dead. Sin had rendered all mankind utterly unable to do anything to please God and achieve redemption. It was said that mankind was not even capable of bringing himself to a place where he may believe. Only the ones whom the Father draws will come.

Grace and Faith. The means whereby man could experience redemption was solely the unsolicited act of God towards those whom he had chosen. Grace was the prospect of a relationship with God that would persuade the chosen to believe. The act by which mankind would believe is faith, but even that is not a human exercise, it is a divine gift. It is the operation of this faith that marks out the elect from the non-elect.

It appears that when the process is viewed from the perspective of time, the following sequences emerge. Romans 8: 28-33. '*Foreknew, predestined, called, justified, and glorified.*'
Ephesians 1: 3-6. '*Chose, predestined, redeemed.*' They are not exactly the same but are easily merged together. It seems by a cursory overview that this is what the text is trying to convey. All this is, we are asked to believe, is, *soli Deo gloria*, for the Glory of God alone.

Divine Sovereignty. The triumphal tones of Romans 8:31-39; 9:14-24, introduce us to the understanding of the Sovereignty of God.
These verses reveal God as absolutely sovereign. He can do whatever he chooses and cannot be charged with inconsistency. Nothing could exist without his creative acts and so he has power over creation to do with it as he wishes, as the potter has power over the clay. He can love Jacob and hate Esau and neither Jacob or Esau can complain.

This sovereignty also applies to the process of salvation and the means whereby it is applied. God chose without consultation to provide the means of redemption. Therefore, it is argued, that he can impose the mechanism and the boundaries of redemption as he pleases. It appears the choices that God makes are not determined by any other thing apart from his own glory. It has been said that both those chosen to benefit from his redemptive acts, and those who do not, are displaying the glory of God, in different ways.

> *Grace has been described as 'God's riches at Christ's expense,' and 'unmerited, undeserved favour.' It is a comprehensive word of boundless reach as it carries an infinite depth of significance indicating unlimited favour to the undeserving: all who by reason of transgressions have forfeited every claim to favour, and have lost all capacity to meritorious action. Grace is the benignity of parental love and the grounds on which God saves men. Grace is free, a favour manifest in the gift of God's Son, and the blessings of salvation through his sacrifice upon the cross. The scriptural definition of Grace will never be improved.*[4]

> *But when the kindness and the love of God our Saviour toward man appeared, not by works of righteousness which we have done, but according to His mercy He saved us, through the washing of regeneration and renewing of the Holy Spirit.* Titus 3:4-5.

---

[4] All the Doctrines of the Bible, Herbert Lockyer

CHAPTER TWO

Grace: the first Christians

In the next few chapters, we are going to examine the development of the understanding of Grace as it has come down to us through the history of the church. We will examine how the difficulties concerning Grace have been dealt with through history, and how and why there are still diverse opinions on the subject. At the end I will present what I believe to be the best understanding of Grace from my convictions based on the Holy Scriptures.

In this chapter we are going to look at how the first generations of believers after the eyewitnesses understood God's Grace. We will do this by quoting from their surviving manuscripts, and how their belief contributed to the formulation of the Doctrine of Grace. We must make it clear that we are speaking about the church as it emerged from the former Roman Empire, and dominated Western Europe, and wherever the European explorers travelled and established colonies. The church in Eastern Europe and Russia, developed along different lines from the time of Constantine in the 4th century.

This is not an appeal to tradition to establish truth. We can see what the Apostles and their companions preached and wrote in the text of the New Testament. But what it meant to those who first heard it and how they applied it, is another matter entirely.

We can approach the subject armed with our Greek, Hebrew, and Latin dictionaries. As valuable as they are, we know, that will only give us the meaning of a word, not a word in the context in which it is written, or with the inspiration and emotion with which it was chosen. One of the clearest ways of trying to understand what was meant is to examine how the gospel was first *heard* and how the apostles' manuscripts were interpreted by those who first received them.

As it has turned out there remains a wealth of documents that contain this information. We will look at some comments by the more notable figures of the 2nd, 3rd and 4th centuries. There were hundreds of such witnesses but I have chosen the more prominent ones. They had received the same text as we have, but what did they make of it?

After all, as in cases of men such as Ignatius and Polycarp, they actually knew the eyewitnesses, and held in their hand, at least some of the autographs. The period of time in which these men lived is noted in the references.

These early Christian leaders mainly focused on the needs of their day, noting that largely their congregations were new converts, and not people born into the faith. Subsequently the emphasis is against idolatry and wanton living and a call to live a life reflective of the Holiness of God. From their quotations, it seems, they were all quite familiar with the vast majority of the New Testament as it exists today, even though there was no closed 'canon.' They viewed the writings of the apostles and their companions as scripture, and as equal to, and illuminating of, the Jewish Scriptures.

> *'Look carefully into the Scriptures, which are the true utterances of the Holy Spirit. Observe that nothing of an unjust or counterfeit character is written in them.'* [5]

Reading through the manuscripts that have survived from this period we can gain the following perspective of the things believed. I have included a rather lengthy list of quotations on the different aspects of Grace.

Firstly, quotations in regard to human inability.

> *Polycarp alludes to 1 Peter 1:8 and then declares, 'knowing that by grace you have been saved, not because of works, by the will of God through Jesus Christ.'* [6]

> *The guarantee of our righteousness is 'Christ Jesus, who bore our sins in his own body upon the tree. Jesus committed no sin and no deceit was found in his mouth. Rather for our sakes he endured all things, in order that we might live in him.'* [7]

It can be deduced from these quotes that Polycarp understood that Salvation was a work of God, complete through Jesus Christ, and no human effort made could make any contribution. Although these words are very similar to the text of Scripture, they are in fact his own words. The following quotations emphasise the same point.

> *Carnal men can no more do the works of the spirit than those who walk in the spirit do the things of the flesh nor can faith do the things of infidelity nor infidelity the things of faith. Since you do all things in Jesus Christ and even those things are spiritual which you do according to the flesh. Clearly then without union with Jesus Christ it would be impossible to act spiritually and*

---

[5] Clement.35-101. (Philippians 4:3) 1 Corinthians 45
[6] Polycarp's 69-156 Letter to the Philippians 3:1.
[7] Ibid 8:1

therefore, please God, because those who are in Christ live a life of faith that is radically different from that of those who do not. [8]

Mankind by Adam fell under death, and the deception of the serpent; we are born sinners ... No good thing dwells in us ... For neither by nature, nor by human understanding is it possible for me to acquire the knowledge of things so great and so divine, but by the energy of the Divine Spirit ... Of ourselves it is impossible to enter the kingdom of God ... He has convicted us of the impossibility of our nature to obtain life ... Free will has destroyed us; we who were free are become slaves and for our sin are sold ... Being pressed down by our sins, we cannot move upward toward God; we are like birds who have wings, but are unable to fly. [9]

His cross, and his death, and his resurrection, and the faith which is through him, are my unpolluted <u>entitlement</u> *(translation mine); and in these, through your prayers, I am willing to be justified.* [10]

Justification by Faith in the work of Christ alone.

'And we, therefore are not justified of ourselves or by our wisdom or insight or religious devotion or the holy deeds we have done from the heart, but by that faith by which almighty God has justified all men from the very beginning. [11]

Through faith, without the works of the law, the dying thief was justified, because the Lord inquired not what he had previously wrought, nor yet waited for his performance of some work after he should have believed; but he took him unto himself for a companion, justified through his confession alone. [12]

---

[8] Ignatius of Antioch.35-107 108-140
[9] Justin Martyr 100-165

[10] Ignatius: Epistle to Philadelphians
[11] Clement 1 Corinthians 32:4.

When an ungodly man is converted, God justified him through faith alone, not on account of good works which he possessed not.[13]

Predestination and Foreknowledge.

God predetermining all things for the perfection of man, and for the bringing about and manifestation of his dispositions, that goodness may be shown, and righteousness perfected, and the church be conformed to the image of his Son, and at length become a perfect man, and by such things be made ripe to see God, and enjoy him.[14]

He asserts a preparation of happiness for some, and of punishment for others, upon the prescience or foreknowledge of God; his words are these, God foreknowing all things, has prepared for both suitable habitations.[15]

We have learned from the prophets and we hold it as true that punishments and chastisements and good rewards are distributed according to the merit of each man's actions. Were this not the case, and were all things to happen according to the decree of fate, there would be nothing at all in our power. If fate decrees that this man is to be good and that one wicked, then neither is the former to be praised nor the latter to be blamed.[16]

God, wishing men and angels to follow his will, resolved to create them free to do righteousness. But if the Word of God foretells that some angels and men shall certainly be punished, it did so because it foreknew that they would be unchangeably wicked, but not because God created them so. So, if they repent all who

---

[12] Origen 184-253.

[13] Jerome 347-420.

[14] Irenaeus against heresies. 50:4, 72, p. 419.

[15] Irenaeus against heresies. 50:4, 76, p. 423

[16] Justin the Martyr 100-1656. Apology 1:43

wish for it can obtain mercy from God.[17]

If then it were not in our power to do or not to do these things, what reason had the apostle, and much more the Lord Himself, to give counsel to do some things and to abstain from others? But because man is possessed of free-will from the beginning, and God is possessed of free-will in whose likeness man was created, advice is always given to him to keep fast the good, which thing is done by means of obedience to God.[18]

It certainly seems from these quotes that the predominant view was that God has foreseen the unfolding events of time before the world began. They believed in the Universal sin of man passed on from Adam. In particular he was aware of who would believe and not believe. God had bestowed on man a capacity of free-will to choose whether to believe or not. God prepared destinies suitable for the souls of the believer and unbeliever respectively.

Universal Atonement.

It seems clear that the gospel was preached to all, believing that all people had the opportunity and responsibility to believe the gospel. Irrespective of the belief in predestination, the decision to believe was made by the free-will of the person concerned.

Jerome explicitly addresses ideas associated with limited atonement—that there are some sins which Christ cannot cleanse and sinners for whom Christ did not die—and treats it as heresy. In refutation of such thinking, he contends, "What else is this but to say that Christ has died in vain? He has indeed died in vain if there are any whom he cannot make alive.[19]

---

[17] Dialogue cxli Justin the Martyr dialogue with Trypho

[18] Irenaeus Against heresies 37.

[19] Jerome, in a letter to the Roman nobleman Oceanus,

Clement says that Christ's sacrifice 'won for the whole world the grace of repentance,' and that 'from generation to generation the Master has given an opportunity for repentance to those who desire to turn to him.' God's offer of repentance and salvation, along with the ability to respond to that offer, are thus envisioned as universal and unlimited, rather than based on a prior, unconditional decree to save some individuals.[20]

Christian Conduct.

Those who are found not living as he taught should know that they are not really Christians, even if his teachings are on their lips, for he said that not those who merely profess but those who also do the works will be saved. [21]

'But to the righteous and holy, and those who have kept his commandments and have remained in his love...he will by his grace give life incorrupt, and will clothe them with eternal glory. [22]

This also shows a recognition that sin was not only what was received from Adam but also what individuals had committed themselves. We could continue but I think that is sufficient to establish an overview of what was believed on the subject we are dealing with. We may summarise it as follows.

Grace was necessary because mankind was rendered by sin, unable in and of himself, to attain to a status of righteousness. A state he had inherited from Adam. Man needed to be enabled.

Grace and faith were the sole unaided factors in the provision of salvation for all mankind.

Grace was displayed when God chose from the masses of

---

[20] 1 Clement 7: 4-7.

[21] Justin the Martyr. Apology 1:16.

[22] Irenaeus. Against heresies 10:1.

humanity, certain ones to be the beneficiaries of that Grace. God foreknew those who his Grace would enable to believe and those it would not.

Grace was evident when those who had been raised to step into a place of righteousness found themselves enabled to continue in that Grace throughout their lives.

The singular, supreme demonstration of Grace was through the death, burial, and resurrection of Jesus Christ.

The Grace that initially saved, and the Grace that caused them to persevere, would, with utter certainty, bring them to Everlasting Life.

From the surviving correspondence from this era, it seems that great emphasis was placed on the character and moral conduct of those who had been baptised. It seems to be of the utmost importance that converts disassociated themselves from any pagan religious practices they were previously involved in. As a result of these beliefs, a convert was expected to display the following;

An attitude of humility that their salvation was undeserved and unmerited. It was important that it was understood that whatever good they had done had no bearing on their salvation. It was entirely the work of Christ. Likewise, no matter how sinful they had been, the atonement of Christ was sufficient to cleanse from all sin.

An understanding that the Grace they had received was to be the motivation to produce similar acts of Grace to others. It was expected that the convert would set out on a journey of faith to become more Christlike. However, whatever they attained would still be a work of undeserved Grace so that all the glory would go to God.

The Sacraments.

In this early period, the church practised two sacraments. Baptism and the Eucharist. They were both seen as commands from the scriptures. They were regarded as symbolic acts with a spiritual significance.

Baptism

> *1. And concerning baptism: Having first said all these things, baptize into the name of the Father, and of the Son, and of the Holy Spirit, in living water.*
> *2. But if there is no flowing water, baptize into other water; in cold or in warm.*
> *3. But if you have not either, pour out water three times upon the head into the name of Father and Son and Holy Spirit.*
> *4. But before the baptism let the baptizer fast, and the baptized, and whatever others can; but order the baptized to fast one or two days before.*[23]

This indicates that a sincere, heartfelt and public repentance was to be made, and wherever possible, accompanied by baptism by immersion. It implies that the persons who were baptised were able to understand what they were doing. This was seen as an expression of faith in the work of Christ on the Cross. By baptism they had symbolically followed the Lord through death into newness of life. They now stood in the Grace of God and their sins were forgiven.

The Eucharist.

Here is a description of the Eucharist in the early second century from Justin the martyr.

> *'Having ended the prayers, we salute one another with a kiss. There is then brought to the president of the brethren*

---

[23] Teaching of the Twelve Apostles, The Didache. Circa 120.

bread and a cup of wine mixed with water; and he taking them, gives praise and glory to the Father of the universe, through the name of the Son and of the Holy Ghost, and offers thanks at considerable length for our being counted worthy to receive these things at His hands. And when he has concluded the prayers and thanksgivings, all the people present express their assent by saying Amen. This word Amen answers in the Hebrew language. And when the president has given thanks, and all the people have expressed their assent, those who are called by us deacons give to each of those present to partake of the bread and wine mixed with water over which the thanksgiving was pronounced, and to those who are absent they carry away a portion.' [24]

For many of us it would not be in anyway strange to step back into a scene like this. It seems that the Eucharist was another form of confession, as the confession of sins was required before participation. As such, to take the bread and wine was to receive the Grace of the Lord Jesus.

But every Lord's Day gather yourselves together, and break bread, and give thanksgiving after having confessed your transgressions, that your sacrifice may be pure. [25]
Not as common bread and common drink do we receive these; but in like manner as Jesus Christ our Saviour, having been made flesh by the Word of God, had both flesh and blood for our salvation, so likewise have we been taught that the food which is blessed by the prayer of His word, and from which our blood and flesh by transmutation are nourished, is the flesh and blood of that Jesus who was made flesh. [26]

A careful reading shows that what is meant is not that the bread and wine were transmuted, but as ordinary food is

---

[24] Documents of the Christian Church Henry Bettenson.
[25] Ibid.
[26] Justin the Martyr.

transmuted to give physical energy, so participating in the eucharist gave spiritual energy to do the will of God.

The bread which our Christ gave us to offer in remembrance of the Body which He assumed for the sake of those who believe in Him, for whom He also suffered, and also to the cup which He taught us to offer in the Eucharist, in commemoration of His blood. [27]

Having taken the bread and given it to His disciples, Jesus made it His own body, by saying, 'This is My body,' that is, the symbol of My body. There could not have been a symbol, however, unless there was first a true body. An empty thing or phantom is incapable of a symbol. He likewise, when mentioning the cup and making the new covenant to be sealed 'in His blood,' affirms the reality of His body. For no blood can belong to a body that is not a body of flesh. [28]

The early Fathers did not seem to 'systemize' the points of belief to any great degree. They were well aware of the dilemma in regard to choosing and not choosing; man's will and God's will; works for salvation and works as a result of salvation. But rather than seeking to explain them, they were wrapped up in the 'Mysteries of the Divine Will' and the matter left at that.

During this period the '*Charismata* ' that was evident in the ministry of the Apostles continued. The working of miracles, casting out of demons, speaking in tongues, and inspired prophecies were well known. These manifestations were seen as the proof of the resurrection of Christ from the dead, which was the central theme of preaching. All these things were seen as the manifestation of the Grace of God among them.[29]

---

[27] Ibid. Dialogue with Trypho the Jew.
[28] Tertullian 160-225. Against Maricon.4:40
[29] Dr William Kay. The Unfailing Stream.

The Grace Space

CHAPTER THREE

Grace: the winds of change

The winds of Change.

In these early years of Christianity, the church, sadly, was not one homogeneous group. There were many 'Christianity's.' Similar to today however, there was a mainstream that was faithful to the teaching of the Apostles.

As the years went by changes began to take place in the churches. These were brought about by both internal and external pressures. Of significance was that there were more 'generational believers,' that is, those born and raised within the faith, than new converts. The generational believers, either in a heartfelt way or by ritual, had developed a pattern of worship by simple repetition. Converts were encouraged to adopt the procedure that was practiced. These procedures then became 'sacred' or sacramental. Gradually these sacraments became the enforced law of the church.

The idea of sacrament also encompassed the idea of mystery. When a sacrament was properly encountered, a mysterious act of the exchange of Grace took place between God and man. This exchange was unexplainable but was understood as the ongoing work of the Holy Spirit in the believer. As we have seen, in the New Testament we find two practices clearly explained, that can be regarded as sacraments, namely, Baptism in water and the Eucharist. These were the first sacraments practised in the church. These are symbolic acts depicting the process of conversion, and the union with Christ, respectively. Baptism is done once, because what it symbolises can only happen once; the Eucharist may be done as often as one wishes because it symbolises the ongoing life of the believer in relation to Jesus Christ.

In this period, the 2nd and 3rd centuries, the church began to go beyond this. The process began with the formation of a hierarchical structure to the church. Each congregation was initially led by a number of presbyters or elders. As the number of churches grew in a certain area it became necessary to co-ordinate practices and agree on doctrine. In order to do this 'councils' or 'synods' were formed. Here representatives of the churches met together to sort things out. These representatives gradually assumed a higher status than the presbyters and became known as bishops. The bishops in turn needed a chairman, and so a 'Metropolitan Bishop' was appointed. Although these appointments were initially simply practical arrangements, they soon obtained official status. It was not unknown for Metropolitan Bishops to be known as 'father, papa or pope,' but this only applied in the area where they operated. This process evolved to include men with wider and wider responsibilities until eventually we have archbishops, cardinals and the supreme father, the Pope. This supreme position settled on the Bishop of Rome simply because Rome was the principal city. Such a title was probably first used in a universal sense, although without the authority, by Siricius 384-399.[30] The first 'head of the church,' the *Pontificus Maximus,* was the emperor Constantine, when he declared Christianity to be the religion of the empire in the 4th century. We will come back to this later. After his death the bishops of Rome seized the title for themselves. All attempts to link this event with Peter as a founding pope require a fair bit of imagination. Even if Matthew 16:18 refers to Peter personally, there is nothing there to empower him to start a dynasty or assume primacy. [31]

The upshot of it all was that a sufficiently persuasive narrative was tabled to show that the papal figure became the representative of Christ on earth, in the same way that Christ had been the representative of the Father. His power was filtered through the hierarchy of the church until it reached the humble communicant. The road was now paved that would lead to the situation, where the humble communicant, could only experience the Grace of God, as it was deemed appropriate to dispense it, by the officers of the church.

It was believed that by participating in the panoply of sacraments, a person maintained their position in the Grace of God. Naturally the main point was that the believer could not gain or hold on to their salvation by anything they could do. It was a matter of Grace. Now that Grace was solely dispensed at the discretion of the Church.

> *If someone from this group of people wants to be saved, let him come into this house so that he may be able to attain his salvation. Let no one, then, be persuaded otherwise, nor let anyone deceive himself. Outside of this house, that is, outside of the Church, no one is saved; for, if anyone should go out of it, he is guilty of his own death.[32]*

---

[30] Millers Church History
[31] The Vicars of Christ. Peter de Rosa. page 33
[32] Origen.250. Homilies on Joshua 3:5.

It must be understood that originally statements such as this were to guard against heresies and the preaching of a gospel contrary to the New Testament. However, they eventually became a threatening spectre, overshadowing anyone who dared to think outside the box. The point was, that even though it was stated that salvation came from Christ, in practice, it was dispensed through the representatives of the church.

Symbolism became the hallmark of the whole thing. The sacraments symbolised in prescribed action what was taught and practiced in scripture. I would humbly point out that there is a huge difference in symbolising something and actually experiencing it. The church began to merge the symbolism with actual experience. If the symbolic act was performed precisely, the spiritual encounter was deemed to have occurred. The communicant could not be allowed to experience anything from any other source, because that would give an individual direct communication with God. The communicant had to become totally dependent on the Church and its officers for Grace, as the Church deemed it appropriate to distribute it.

We are now going to look at the form of sacraments that emerged that superseded the first beliefs about Baptism and the Eucharist, and that have to do with the dispensing of Grace.

Baptism and Confirmation.

The dispensing of Grace began at birth. During this time baptism was changed from an act of confession and commitment by someone able to understand what they were doing, to an act of securing one's membership of the Christian family. The 'baptism' cleansed the child from the inherited sins from Adam. Instead of the act of baptism following a time of instruction in the faith, the instruction followed baptism. When the child was of an age of understanding they confirmed their baptism. As a result, the first step of Grace was administered and the assurance given that if the child had died in infancy, it would not have been lost.

As this form of baptism symbolised conversion, so confirmation symbolised the filling with the Holy Spirit. The person sins were declared forgiven and the Holy Spirit declared conferred whether anything spiritual actually happened to the individual or not.

Confession and Penance

Having obtained absolution for inherited sin the next problem was how to obtain Grace for personal sin. This was dealt with by confessing to a priest, who would forgive your sin, on God's behalf, at the imposition of an arduous task. The arduous task was designed to bring humility and was a punitive measure to 'pay' for the cost of the sins confessed. By so doing another measure of Grace was dispensed to cover the misdemeanours concerned. This was an ongoing procedure.

Extreme Unction and Purgatory.

None of these procedures happened over night. They all were first practiced in a local, *ad hoc,* way, as someone came up with the idea, and gradually spread and gained acceptance until they were made the official position of the church. Extreme Unction was also called *'The sacrament of the Anointing of the Sick*' and was originally recognised in the 12th century. It also became known as the 'last rites.' The sacrament of Purgatory was officially recognised much earlier, in the 7th century. It is better known as The Sacrament of Reconciliation.

It was realised that everyone did not remember every sin and did not always act honestly at the confessional. There were many sins that were committed that were not confessed. As the baptism sealed the person as a Christian and guaranteed eternal life, something further was required to cleanse those who reached the end of their lives without the Grace of total forgiveness.

Extreme Unction was called 'extreme' because it came at the extremity of life, the moment of death. If the person made full and final confession of all sins, absolution could be granted by a priest on behalf of the Church. But not all moments of death were cognitive moments. And because it was at the end of life, no penance could be imposed.

So, the idea of Purgatory was conceived. This was an indefinite period of purging in the after-life that prepared a person for heaven. 1 Corinthians 3:11-15 was developed to formulate the concept.

This became the real iron fist of the medieval church and the thing that held the people in fear. In some locations it still does. Who entered and who exited Purgatory, and how long they were there, was at the discretion of the Church, and the Pope in particular. As a result, people were never really sure that they or their loved one's had received sufficient Grace to enter heaven. It was always maintained that the forgiveness of sins was obtainable only through the death and resurrection of Jesus, but that the Grace that was obtained, was only given through the auspices of the church.

Purgatory.

Purgatory was dealt with through Invocations and Indulgences. Invocations are prayers of humility declaring dependence on the mercy of God. They could be offered for oneself or others.
Loved ones were expected to offer prayers to the Saints to aid their loved ones through the process of purging. It was

believed that the saints were so holy they had accumulated a 'surplus of grace' that they could share with weaker believers. To facilitate this transfer, they were expected to venerate the saints, offer donations, fasting, prayers, and engage in acts that caused suffering to themselves, in order that the Grace the penance obtained, could be shared with the departed to speed their journey to heaven.

These indulgencies became official church practice in the 11th century. Indulgencies were carefully calculated in proportion to the piety shown. That is, the more arduous the task the more Grace was released. None of these institutions were available without the payment of a fee or a donation of some kind.

> *All who die in God's grace and friendship, but still imperfectly purified, are indeed assured of their eternal salvation; but after death they undergo purification, so as to achieve the holiness necessary to enter the joy of heaven.*
> *The Church gives the name Purgatory to this final purification of the elect, which is entirely different from the punishment of the damned.*
> *The Church formulated her doctrine of faith on Purgatory at the Councils of Florence and Trent.* [33]

The Eucharist

Many of the Fathers whom we will often quote, seemed to believe that the wine and bread were miraculously transformed into the body and blood of the Lord. However, we must be cautious here and not interpret the pastoral comments of the Fathers by the scholastic definitions of later times.

What is clear is that it was believed that to take the Eucharist or Thanksgiving, was a sacred act. In some form or other

---

[33] Catholic Answers. www.Catholic.com

Christ was present in the bread and wine. They clearly state that there is a correlation between 'bread' and 'body' and 'wine' and 'blood.' It all emanates from Luke 22: 19-20. The influencers of the Church began to conflate things said figuratively and literally, and came up with conclusion that the bread and wine were transformed into the actual blood and body of the Lord. They claimed that the celebration of the Eucharist involved the real presence of Christ. By 'real' they meant 'physical.' They began to teach that at the prayer of consecration this irreversible change of substance took place and they were now handling the actual body and blood of the Lord. This is not what the early Fathers had taught as we have noted previously.

Origen Adamantius of Alexandria (184-253) draws on several biblical passages to confirm that the Eucharist was representative, spiritual and figurative, not the physical body and blood of the Lord. From Matthew 15:17-20, he points out the difference between the spiritual and the natural elements in eating, both a meal, and the Eucharist. He places emphasis on the spiritual.

> *Now, if everything that enters into the mouth goes into the belly and is cast out into the drought, even the meat which has been sanctified through the word of God and prayer, in accordance with the fact that it is material, goes into the belly and is cast out into the draught, but in respect of the prayer which comes upon it, according to the proportion of the faith, becomes a benefit and is a means of clear vision to the mind which looks to that which is beneficial, and it is not the material of the bread but the word which is said over it which is of advantage to him who eats it not unworthily of the Lord. And these things indeed are said of the typical and symbolical body.*[34]

> *As another example, take the Lord's words, The bread that I shall give for the life of the world is my flesh. When the Jews*

---

[34] Origen Commentary on Mathew.

strove with one another saying, how can this man give us his flesh to eat? we showed that the hearers were not so foolish as to suppose that the speaker was inviting the hearers to approach him and eat of his flesh. [85]

He refers to 2 Corinthians 3:6 and emphasises the need to see the spiritual overtones or biblical terminology.

Know that they are figures written in the divine volumes and, for that reason, examine and understand what is said as spiritual and not as carnal. For if you receive those things as carnal, they wound you and do not sustain you. For even in the Gospels, it is the letter that kills. Not only in the Old Testament is the letter that kills found; there is also in the New Testament the letter that kills that one who does not spiritually perceive what is said. For, if you follow according to the letter that which is said, unless you eat my flesh and drink my blood, this letter kills. [36]

The early Church fathers very clearly believed in the real presence of Christ at the Eucharist, but this did not mean they believed the bread and wine became the actual body and blood of the Lord. I believe it was clear to the Fathers that the prayer of invocation or consecration did not change the substance of the bread and wine, but changed the significance. They were remembering his death, giving thanks for salvation, celebrating his victory over death, and proclaiming the unity of the church, the body of Christ. The entire experience was to create an atmosphere where the participant could say, '*We were there.*' (At calvary) Any Grace or virtue gained from the Eucharist was obtained by the believing heart of the participant reaching out to God through faith. The real presence of Christ is there. But the real presence of Christ was there when they gathered, Matthew 18:20; when they worshipped, Psalm 22:3; in the preaching of the word, 1 Corinthians 1:23; and as they journeyed

---

[35] Origen. Commentary on John
[36] Origen Homilies on Leviticus

through life, Matthew 28: 20; John 14:3. The whole purpose was to transform the participant from sinfulness to holiness, not to transform the bread and wine.

However, in its desire to be the mediator between God and man, the Church was not satisfied with this arrangement. It allowed the communicant to potentially experience the Presence of God individually and internally without the auspices of the Church.

The Eucharist came to be seen as an essential part of the chain of sacraments by which participants could obtain Grace from God. Confession, penance and the Eucharist are closely linked, distinguishable by degree of solemnity. Confession and penance prepared one for the Eucharist. The Eucharist was the re-enacted sacrifice of Christ. His body is broken again and his blood is shed again to cleanse the sins of the participants. Taking the bread displays that the participant is now one with Christ and all sins are forgiven up to that moment. The system was careful never to offer complete assurance of everlasting life so that the person would forever be dependent on the church for salvation.

In the course of time the Church compiled laws that forbade any substance except wheat bread, wine mixed with water, the laity could only receive the bread, anything leftover is consumed by the Priest.

The Mystery of Confession or more correctly Reconciliation restores the originally cleansing of Baptism by mechanism of the indwelling of the Holy Spirit. By Synergy with the Grace of the Mysteries, we are cleansed of Sin and restored, reconciled back to Christ. This is finalized through receiving His Body and Blood. It is a cycle, like all matters of life, to encourage this gradual healing, this synergy of the Holy Spirit, this Theosis [37] of

---

[37] A transformation to Christlikeness.

Salvation. [38]

The Church was now set on a course that would lead it further and further away from the scriptures and create the great monolith that dominated the western world for a thousand years. Of course, there were exceptions. There were always men and women of faith who found a dynamic relationship with God by the Holy Spirit, but overall, the trend was set.

I would say that it is important to differentiate between the opinion of the early church Fathers, 90-150, who represented the first and second generation after the eyewitnesses, and the later Fathers who began to develop the traditions we have spoken about.
This understanding of Grace prevailed for a couple of hundred years or so, and would have no doubt continued for longer, were it not for the arrival of a man called Constantine.

---

[38] Forums.orthodox christinaity

The Grace Space

CHAPTER FOUR.

Grace: in the hands of the scholars

A further significant change began to evolve in the Church by the emergence of the scholars. There had been scholars all along, such as Origen and Eusebius, but the testimony of the church had largely been carried by the Fathers whose foundations were scriptural and hearts pastoral. Now the matters of doctrine passed to the hands of scholars. They were distinguished from the Fathers because they were well versed, not only in the languages of the Biblical text, but also in the philosophies, particularly, of Plato and Aristotle. The philosophical training made it necessary to 'tie up the loose ends' of theology which the Fathers had left in 'the mysteries,' by producing theology in a systemised, philosophical way.

Flavius Valerius Constantinus; Constantine. 272-337; emperor 306-337.

After gaining the position of emperor, Constantine was

disposed to offer recognition to Christianity. He felt the Christian God had favoured him in obtaining the position so he was prepared to bring a halt to the persecution of the Church and make Christianity an official religion of the empire. Persecution had prevailed, to a greater or lesser extent since the apostles. Different geographical areas were less tolerant than others. A particular severe period of persecution had preceded Constantine. Initially he only granted Christianity equal status with other religions.

As to his personal faith, there are many questions. He was described as, *'Having a cold and terrible lust for power.'* [39] He was only baptised on his death bed. He was first and foremost a warrior, then a politician, and finally a 'Christian.'

But there was a price to pay for the Church's new found freedoms. Constantine insisted there could be only one form of Christianity in the empire, with a common creed. The church must unify its beliefs and practices. He did this by calling and presiding over a series of church councils. He remained very much the ruler of the church as well as the empire until his transfer to Constantinople in 330. The administrative gap left in Rome by this move, was quickly filled by the new church leaders eager for power and prestige. They adopted the pomp and ceremony of a court and set out to make Rome the capital of a Christian Empire. As a result, Rome became the hub of the church and Constantinople the hub of the empire.

As far as the subject of Grace is concerned the Constantine revolution was, overall, less helpful than helpful. Street battles ensued over the election of bishops, evangelism turned into debates, and sometimes open conflict, over preciseness of doctrine. Lifestyles were far from the scriptural standards, but consciences were eased through the sacramental system.

---

[39] The Age of Constantine the Great. Jacob Buerckhardt

There were pious laity and clergy dotted around the empire who still kept a flame of Biblical Christianity burning, but the overall trend was very dark indeed.

The Great Councils.

Constantine was responsible for setting up many such councils in this period. They were mostly concerning matters such as; the humanity and deity of Jesus, the Trinity, the date of Easter, and the canonisation of the documents of the bible, but they also endorsed the sacramental system and added to its complexity.

What the councils managed to do as well was to draw a sharp line between what was to be considered heresy and orthodoxy. It now became fashionable to denounce people who would not toe the orthodox line and excommunicate them from the church. Excommunication meant exile from their sphere of influence, and being refused participation in the sacraments. This of course meant a withholding of Grace, in the day, a fearful predicament. Most of the early excommunications were to do with a person's views on the Trinity and the humanity/divinity of Jesus. The theological framework for condemning heretics was devised by Augustine and the first executions were carried out under Emperor Maximus in 385.

Pelagius 354-418.

Pelagius came on the scene and stirred things up by introducing a novel theory regarding the process of salvation and what was meant by Grace. His ideas hit at the heart of the sacramental system and hence the authority of the Church.

Pelagius turned the whole thing upside down by declaring a set of beliefs that placed the obtaining and maintaining of salvation squarely in the hands of mankind himself, thus negating altogether the sacramental system.

He was essentially concerned with the depravity that had crept into the church. He saw Grace as dispensed in the sacraments as an excuse for further immorality. Basically, to him, it appeared that, you could live how you wished and the sacramental system would take care of everything.

Consequently, he denied universal sin inherited from Adam. He argued that if the root of sin in humanity was the fault of Adam, then individuals could not be held responsible. He said Adam's only role was to set a bad example and so teach humanity that it was possible to choose to sin. A person's sin was as a result of their own actions.

He pointed out that man was morally neutral and that he was created 'good,' and was therefore inherently good. Grace to Pelagius was the God given ability to choose to do good. He denied the need for any divine intervention of Grace in conversion. To him it was a matter of the human self-determination. He advocated that salvation was to live a holy life achieved by a rigid obedience to the moral law. In this he was distinctly 'Pharisaic.' To follow Pelagius's ideas through it would mean that man could attain righteousness simply by making his own right decisions.

The place Pelagius gave to Jesus Christ in salvation is somewhat vague, but it seems to settle on the idea that Jesus showed it was possible to choose the will of God as Adam had shown it was possible to do the opposite. The example of Jesus supposedly inspired the ability in followers to make similar choices.

He was eventually excommunicated, but the damage was done. Pelagius had tapped into a fundamental need in the structure of human nature, the need to *do* something rather than have something presented to you as a gift; the feeling of autonomy, not dependence on anyone, including God; the sense of self-sufficiency, and the satisfaction of a job well done. A '*Pandora's box*' had been opened which would just not close again. I fear mankind is Pelagian at heart.[40]

Pelagius had the effect of galvanising into action one of the most renowned scholars in church history, Augustine of Hippo.[41] Augustine, up until this point, had gone along happily with the accepted position on Grace as described earlier. He saw Pelagius as the nemesis of truth and devoted his later years to denouncing him.

In opposing Pelagius, he deemed it necessary to produce a 'systematic theology' that explained all the dilemmas and could be used to crush all error, both evident and potential. It would also draw the line between truth and error. He achieved it by employing philosophic methods to join together the dots of scripture. He was particularly influenced by the methods of Plato and Aristotle. He was the first, and possibly the greatest of the Scholars.

Augustine of Hippo. 354-430

Augustine wrote and preached extensively covering all aspects of doctrine, practice and governance of society. His thinking linked up the 'loose ends of the Church Fathers' theology. For our purpose we are only interested in how Augustine dealt with Grace and what he did with the common beliefs he inherited from the Fathers and which Pelagius had desecrated.

To try and reduce Augustine into a few simple statements is rather like trying to pour the Atlantic Ocean into a bottle. He

---

[40] Joseph Lupi St Augustine's Doctrine on Grace
[41] Hippo was a port in what is today Algeria

wrote 100 books, 500 sermons and 200 letters that still exist. It must be pointed out however that Augustine never could read Greek. His knowledge of Greek came from Jerome.

Our inquiry is complicated by the fact there are '*two Augustines.*' The first is the one venerated by Catholic commentators as the single most influential writer in Christendom, defender of the true church and its traditions, second only to the Biblical authors themselves. The other is the one interpreted by the later Protestant Reformers, who attempted to deconstruct Catholic superstition and return us to the true understanding of scripture. Augustine was the father of both.

A further complication is that there were many manuscripts that were falsely attributed to Augustine that gave theological views with which Augustine did not ascribe.

Augustine's theological motivations were doubtlessly influenced by his association with a group called the Manicheans [42] with whom he spent nine years. Although he later vehemently rejected their overall teaching, their influence in certain aspects of his thought, evidently remained. [43] These would include the emphasis on the total depravity of mankind and the idea of a closed number of elect. Where Augustine differed was with the teaching of the Manicheans that said Light and Darkness were two opposing eternal 'gods', whereas Augustine made God the author of good and the permitter of evil.

Augustine is revered and renowned as a great philosopher, who influenced, not only the Medieval Church but western society in general, to the present day. But, like us all, he had feet of clay. He did not only write with a focus on making God

---

[42] Followers of Mani. 216-274.
[43] Exploring Manichaeism. K Samples.

and the scriptures known, but was also very much a reactionary to the world in which he lived.

- He was fixated on refuting Pelagius.
- He never quite came to assurance of forgiveness for the promiscuity of his adolescence.
- He had to deal with refugees fleeing from the fall of Rome and finding refuge in his community in Northern Africa.

Augustine's theology was shaped by these forces.[44] Augustine must also be accountable for the move that would define authentic Christianity by the preciseness of its creed and the logic of its doctrine, instead of the continuing signs and wonders evidenced in the New Testament.

We have already commented that the specific turning point, if it can be so defined, would be the legalisation of Christianity under Constantine, some 50 years before Augustine. But it was Augustine who finally laid to rest the 'charismata' of the early centuries. As a result, the church was largely, but not absolutely, devoid of its *raison d'etre for* a thousand years or more.[45]

The Sovereignty of God

Augustine believed the starting point of the subject of Grace was understanding the absolute sovereignty of God.

For He is not truly called Almighty if He cannot do whatsoever He pleases, or if the power of His almighty will is hindered by the will of any creature whatsoever.[46]

---

[44] The legacy of Augustine. Kingscollege.net
[45] The Unfailing Stream Dr David Allen.
[46] Nicene and Post Nicene Fathers 1.3, 267)

To Augustine, God was utterly impassive, without expressions of love or hate, compassion or resentment. He acted from the source of pure reason through his sovereign will. The emotions that are employed in scripture to define God are nothing more than anthropomorphisms. An attempt to describe the indescribable. To say that 'God loved the world' or 'God is Love,' is saying in human terms the fact that God chose arbitrarily to show Grace to certain sinners.

Augustine took the position that both the righteous and the unrighteous displayed his glory. The righteous in the benefits of Grace and eternal life, and the unrighteous by bearing his righteous judgements and eventual damnation. Who was to be favoured as righteous and who was to be condemned as unrighteous was a result of his sovereign will?

We need to ask, 'Who was Augustine preaching this to, and why?' In 410 Rome fell to the Visigoths. Some 800 years of Roman history, customs, and beliefs lay in ruins. Refugees came to the enclave of Hippo in North Africa where Augustine resided. Augustine found it important to say, that although the earthly City had fallen there was another City[47] which would never fall, ruled over by a God that would never fail.[48]

So even though it seems that things happen that are contrary to His will, in reality that is only a matter of our perceptions. Everything that happens in the world actually goes exactly according to His plan. He says: "The will of the Omnipotent is never defeated. The omnipotent God never does anything except of His own free-will, and never wills anything that He does not perform."[49]

Intelligent creatures, both angels and humans, sinned—doing

---

[47] Augustine used the term City of God in a way we would use the term Kingdom of God today.

[48] Augustine. City of God Book 5

[49] Nicene and Post Nicene fathers. 1.3, 270 ·

not His will but their own, He used their wilful sin as an instrument for carrying out His will. For in the very fact that they acted in opposition to His will, His will concerning them was fulfilled.[50]

Augustine, in his attempt to give comfort to the refugees, attributed absolute supremacy to God, and inadvertently made God impassionate, remote, untouchable, and to be feared. This was not opposed to the general view of God, that had developed to this point, but the remoteness of God it implied, did have repercussions. It led to the development of more sympathetic intermediaries in the process of dispensing Grace such as, the saints, and, in particular, the Virgin Mary. Not that people were supposed to pray to these people, although that is what it amounted to, but through them, because they understood the frailty of humanity. Even our Lord, *'Touched with the feelings of our infirmities'* was considered too remote. From this position Augustine developed his teachings on Grace.

Original Sin and Human Depravity.

By depravity, Augustine meant, not than man was incapable of doing good and noble things, but that he was incapable of doing anything to obtain God's favour, approval, and salvation. He was particularly emphatic that it was even impossible to choose to do good. This was in order to combat Pelagius. Augustine said that mankind was not so much as able to choose God's Grace when it was presented to him. The will of mankind was warped in original sin and totally depraved. This follows from the views of sovereignty that salvation had to be totally a work of God without the interference of mankind. This Universal Depravity was a result of Adam's sin and was transmitted down through the

---

[50] Ditto 1.3, 269)

generations by procreation.[51]

I am not convinced that Augustine ever truly dealt with the guilt and shame of the waywardness and wastefulness of his youth. It seems that he developed the ideas in order to place the blame for his sin on the state in which he was born, with which he had nothing to do, and to declare a salvation, with which he equally had nothing to do, helped him cope with the guilt and receive the Divine favour without merit or pride.[52]

The remainder now follows quite logically.

Predestination.

Augustine reasoned, as some people actually believe the gospel, their will must have been enabled to believe. God must cause this enabling, as salvation is totally a work of God. Many do not believe the gospel, so their will is not enabled to believe. Therefore, God chose, elected, or predestined the number of those who would be enabled. This was the identity of the Elect. This was a manifestation of Grace in the sense that all men were condemned and God rescued a certain number from eternal judgement.

A Limited Atonement.

Augustine follows on by saying, as God is supremely sovereign his works cannot fail. So, Grace cannot fail. If Grace was made available to all men it would have failed because all men were not saved. Therefore, Grace was only made available to the Elect so it would not fail to produce the desired effect. The Elect, of course, to Augustine were those who held faithfully the Catholic Faith and the traditions of the Fathers as he had

---

[51] Augustine City of God Book 13 Ch.14:

[52] The Confessions of St Augustine.

developed them.

Augustine does not specifically refer to the fate of the 'non-elect' but the logical conclusion of this would be that they were condemned to damnation, to show the glory of God's Justice.

Grace and Perseverance.

Augustine saw Grace as a Gift from God which enabled the person to believe and to persevere in their belief. Because it was a gift of God it could not fail once exercised, and was therefore only given to enable the Elect. Salvation was a process of making a person holy and fit for heaven. Grace came in the accepted ongoing steps we have noted; baptism (infant), confession, penance, and purgatory, until a person was finally purged of all sin and fit for heaven. A person who died in a state of grace would by that achievement define that they were predestined to glory. Committal of a mortal sin, that is a sin committed with intention and disregard of consequence, could cause a person to 'fall from Grace' and be lost. This was explained by saying that in such a case an individual had received saving Grace but not persevering Grace.

As it turned out this aspect of Augustine's teaching was never embraced by the Roman Church. He worked in North Africa and there were times when the relationship with Rome was dislocated.

This aspect of Augustine's teaching hung around, like a slightly distasteful odour, in the halls of scholastic debate, for the next thousand years. His voluminous writings on theology expounding his otherwise orthodox Roman Catholic Convictions, cemented his name forever in the archives of

Church history.[53]

Although Pelagius was denounced as a heretic, Medieval Catholicism found his teaching more advantageous to its purposes. Although it was taught that salvation was entirely a work of God, in practice considerable human effort was demanded to secure that salvation through the rites of penance and the dread of purgatory. Things evolved slowly and selected teachings of the scholars were discussed and endorsed by the popes and so became church law.

The multitudes of people who lived through those times placed their faith in the church and its institutions, believing it was their pathway to eternal life but it was largely an illusion. Step by step the church slumped into an abyss of spiritual irrelevancy, debauchery and superstition, always mindful of how to extract the maximum finances from the masses as possible. [54]

---

[53] Catholic Fidelity.com
[54] The Vicars of Christ. Peter de Rosa.

The Grace Space

CHAPTER FIVE

Grace: the Reformers.

The Reformers. 1509-1609

By the 16th century the Roman Church had reached new depths of depravity. It had become a multi-national institution, economically wealthy, politically invincible and tyrannical. It influenced or controlled the lives of people from humble peasants through to princes, kings and emperors.

The priesthood largely wallowed in debauchery. It determined what was taught in Science, Art and Mathematics as well as religion. It enacted laws and doctrines designed to hold people in fear of eternal damnation and to extract as much wealth as possible from them.

Worship, was to follow the rituals, and there was little concern over the spiritual welfare of individuals. Dissenters were vilified and often executed for heresy. Church laws were based far more on traditions than the word of God, although a text was always contorted to give the appearance of a Biblical basis. The Bible was rarely if ever consulted. The

Church which had formed under the tolerance of Constantine now became the most intolerant institution on earth. Of course, again I emphasise, there were always exceptions. There were pious priests and believers scattered around Christendom who, despite it all, forged a meaningful relationship with God. Yet the church still presented itself as the only means of salvation and God's representative on earth.

The straw that broke the camel's back was the sale of indulgences and ecclesiastical office. We have already explained the basic concept of Purgatory. It was described as the final purging or cleansing of sin that takes place after death but before one enters heaven. Indulgences were a process of prayers for the departed, now sold for money or favour in order for a soul in purgatory to have their 'sentence' reduced or cancelled altogether by the Pope or Bishops. They were sold in the form of certificates. The outstanding punishment was cancelled or reduced by the transfer of excess righteousness accumulated by the saints to the person in question. This excess grace, it was believed, was stored in the 'treasury of the Church,' and was at the discretion of the bishops to share with those not so privileged.

As for ecclesiastical office, positions of authority in the church would be sold to the highest bidder irrespective of their capability to fulfil such an office. The Grace of God was reduced to the whims of the Clergy and was dispensed only by the prescribed acts of penance or the payment of money or favour. This is largely simplified but gives an idea of the world which the Reformers challenged. It had come to the point where anything would be an improvement.

The 16th century was the century of the Reformation. Obviously, it didn't switch on and off like a light. More exactly, there was a sunrise and a sunset; precursors and an aftermath. But that was when the significant action took place. It was a human revolution. It focused on the Bible and what it meant because every area of life was dominated and controlled by an interpretation of the Bible that held the majority of Europe and the colonies, in fear, poverty, ignorance and despair.

This is why many historical commentators identify the reformers as humanists. Humanists, not in the sense it is used today, that is, the attempt to improve the well-being of mankind couched in Atheism or at the best Deism. But an attempt to improve the well-being of mankind by redefining the Christian Dogma under which man was compelled to live. Unlike the later '*Enlightenment*' which sought to lay aside the concept of God all together, the Reformation sought to 'reform' the way the Bible was understood. Christianity and some form of the Christian Church would still remain at the centre of society. The way people lived would be determined by the text of the Bible, not the traditions of the church. That was the goal, whether it was actually achieved or not is another matter. The reformers sought not only to bring people to a biblical understanding of God's Grace, but to also reform society by elevating the dignity and well-being of ordinary people.

The principal reformers, that is, those who took on the Catholic Church face to face, were relatively few, maybe around 20 or so. We are going to look at three. I covered the 'scholastic period' with reference to only two individuals. Pelagius and Augustine. There were many more significant contributors but these two gave us a fair idea of the outcome of the imposition of scholasticism. Likewise, three individuals will give us the necessary overview of the outcome of the Reformation and it's view of Grace.

We are going to consider the works of a first-generation reformer, Martin Luther, a second-generation reformer John Calvin, and a third-generation reformer, Jacobus Arminius. Of course, there were many who climbed aboard the wagon for other reasons than the spiritual. They pursued political, educational, social, military or economical goals. They each used the others influence to gain the advantage.

In England for example, the English reformers saw the matter of the divorce of Henry 8th and the establishment of the Church in England, an opportunity they could not miss in order to gain more spiritual freedoms. King Henry lived and died a 'Catholic at heart,' but the independence of the church was highly beneficial for the reformers. They sided with the King because of the advantages it gained for the cause.

I feel I must say again that when I use the term 'the church in the 16th century' I am generalising. There would always be God-fearing, pious priests, and likewise communicants. The overall scenario was that the church was not presenting the Grace of God at all. The people in general were programmed to believe that their sins were dealt with through the superstitious rituals, and that the priesthood had the power to dispense or withhold Grace, whereas in fact, very little sincere repentance or absolution was taking place. And as for the transference of accumulated Grace from one individual to another, it is pure superstition.

Martin Luther, 1483-1546. John Calvin. 1509-1564.

Luther was one of the first to protest and survive. He was German and a Priest of the Augustinian order and as a result his thoughts were motivated from the writings of Augustine from a thousand years previously. As the Roman Church based its authority on the Church Fathers, Luther saw it as an ideal place to begin, therefore he began to re-interpret the works of Augustine.

We must understand that Luther birthed the Reformation. It was happening within him and around him at the same time.

It was not a done thing from the beginning. He never intended to start a new church, but rather to reform the Catholic Church. Some of his early views were stated differently later on. Here we find, as we once had two '*Augustines*,' we now have two '*Luthers*,' the early one and the later one.

Calvin was a French Theologian and Philosopher. He possessed formidable intellect. He is described as the greatest of the reformers. In fact, Calvin's work so eclipsed the others, many would, even today, erroneously equate Calvinism with Reformed Doctrine, as being one and the same thing.

Luther and Calvin, surprisingly, never met or corresponded, although they were well aware of each other. Calvin thought more of Luther than Luther did of Calvin. [55]

Luther and Calvin generally reached the same conclusions. They both began with the Absolute Sovereignty of God. Nothing could or would happen outside of his will.

> *Let us suppose, for example, that a merchant, after entering a forest in company with trust-worthy individuals, imprudently strays from his companions and wanders bewildered till he falls into a den of robbers and is murdered. His death was not only foreseen by the eye of God, but had been fixed by his decree.*[56]

Calvin's mantra was '*soli Deo Gloria*' [57] Everything was for the Glory of God. Hence Grace, in the first place brought Glory to God, it was only secondarily to relieve a person from the guilt of sin. The rest of their theology emanated from that.

The Grace that brought about Salvation was obtained through faith in the efficacy of the death of Christ. However, both the Grace and the participants in the Grace were pre-determined

---

[55] Luther and Calvin. M L G Sickler.
[56] *John Calvin, Institutes of Christian Religion 1.16.9*
[57] For the Glory of God Alone.

in past ages by God's Eternal Decrees. Who was to be saved and who was to be condemned was decided before any man was born.

A person's salvation began in the arbitrary Election of God and ended in the Predestined place of all so elected. As it was exclusively a work of God, God could do with Grace as he pleased without recourse to anyone. The description of election in Romans 9: 14-24 was interpreted to mean that Grace was only made available to the Elect. Everyone else was condemned to eternal damnation without recourse to appeal.

Like Augustine, Luther declared that the Elect displayed God's Glory through the fact he had chosen them, and the reprobate displayed God Glory in the righteousness of his judgments for sinners. The Divine Will was supreme. There was no such thing as the freedom of human will, the reprobate was bound to choose to sin, and the redeemed were bound to choose righteousness.

In fact, Luther said he personally wrestled with this idea, but nevertheless it was his conclusion as he describes in this startling confession.

Omnipotence and foreknowledge of God, I repeat, utterly destroys the doctrine of 'free-will.' Doubtless it gives the greatest possible offense to common sense or natural reason, that God, who is proclaimed as being full of mercy and goodness, and so on, should of His own mere will abandon, harden and damn men, as though He delighted in the sins and great eternal torments of such poor wretches. It seems an iniquitous, cruel, intolerable thought to think of God; and it is this that has been such a stumbling block to so many great men down through the ages. And who would not stumble at it? I have stumbled at it myself more than once, down to the deepest pit of despair, so that I wished I had never been made a man. That was before I knew how health-giving that despair was, and how close to grace.[58]

It seems as if Luther first recoiled at the horror of the logic of predestination, that millions were damned. Then he saw it as an exposure of the depths of depravity. Then it enabled him to appreciate the privilege he enjoyed as one of the Elect. It's the sad thing about history and the Reformed doctrine, they are both written by the winners!

The Elect were only certain of their election at the end of their life if they had remained faithful. The reason why their thinking went down these lines was to oppose the trend in the Roman Church to practice Pelagius's views, that in practice, a person had to contribute to their salvation. It was deemed necessary to break the tyrannical power the Church exercised over its communicants. Through this system a person could find salvation directly through faith in Jesus Christ and maintain that salvation without the auspices of the church. In this it enjoyed a considerable measure of success.

Luther goes back to endorsing only two sacraments - Baptism and the Eucharist. He introduced the criterion that a sacrament, to be authentic, had to be a direct command from the scriptures. Also, the mere participation in a sacrament, to him, was meaningless, it had to be accompanied by faith of the individual, or the sponsor as in the case of an infant. At baptism the infant received the faith necessary to experience Grace throughout their life. The act of baptism was the act of regeneration and was irrevocable. Again, not by faith in the sacrament, but faith in the work of Christ which the sacrament signified. The bread and wine of the sacrament were indeed the body and blood of the Lord, but only during the moment faith was exercised on the behalf of the communicant. Luther emphasised the vital importance of the spiritual experience above the symbolic act.

---

[58] Luther. Bondage of the Will.

Luther did not reject the other sacraments outright, but relegated them, along with many ecclesiastical practices, to the category of '*indifferences.*' These were defined as practices that did not have any direct bearing on salvation, but could be practiced if it helped one's understanding. Luther showed much more latitude to the '*indifferences*' than Calvin. The distinction between Luther and Calvin is essentially in the way they spoke of these things. Luther was more Pastoral in nature. The triumph of Grace to him was the fact the sinner was justified through Faith. The triumph of Grace for Calvin was that it glorified God.

Luther's preaching was more prophetic, in that it appealed to the heart. Calvin was a scholar and a philosopher of the highest rank. He was totally absorbed in reason, logic, and the 'cause and effect' of theology. Hence, Calvin appealed to, and fascinated the intellect. Luther was more compassionate and appealed more to the ordinary person, whereas Calvin was quite ruthless and clinical. The outcome was more or less the same.

Calvin's theology on Grace has been reproduced and systemised by later followers with the acronym, TULIP.

T stands for Total Depravity. Some sins are worse than others but all sins place mankind under the sentence of Total Depravity. It meant that people could do good things to one another, but as far as salvation was concerned, they could do nothing to stand in the Grace of God. At best, mankind was so depraved that even when presented with the Gospel he had no ability to believe. He could only believe if he was enabled to do so. God only enabled the ones he had chosen. Ephesians 2:1-2.

U stands for Unconditional Election. If the former is true then this logically follows. The enablement was the evidence of Election. God, arbitrarily or unconditionally, chose a certain number to be saved. He paid no attention to who they were, their gifts, talents or abilities, as there could be no trace of human merit in salvation. He just chose them. Those whom he elected would inevitably accept the Gospel and remain in the faith. As those chosen for salvation are predestined to receive eternal life, so those not elected are predestined to eternal damnation by the same decree. Ephesians 1: 4-5.

God preordained, for his own glory and the display of His attributes of mercy and justice, a part of the human race, without any merit of their own, to eternal salvation, and another part, in just punishment of their sin, to eternal damnation.[59]

L stands for Limited Atonement. Jesus died only for the elect. As the will of God was sovereign, Jesus could not die for anyone who would not eventually be saved. He did not die for the whole world because that would mean his death only made salvation possible. He only died for the Elect which made salvation actual.

Christ is the propitiation for our sins; not only ours, but also the sins of the whole world which He hath bought with His blood. 1 John 2:2.

The thing we must remember here is that '*the world*' in this context, meant, to Calvin, the Church in the World.[60] The death of Christ was only effective for the Elect. To be fair, later on, Calvin did say that Christ died for all, but only interceded for the Elect. Frankly I don't see how that changes the outcome.

I stands for Irresistible Grace. Once again this is a logical consequence. Those whom God calls must respond positively because it has been decreed. This is seen as God, not forcing

---

[59] Institutes of the Christian Religion. John Calvin.
[60] voxpatristica.blogspot.com et aL

a person to believe, but making a person willing to believe. Those who resist the call are not among the Elect. John 6: 37.

> *The statement amounts to this, that we ought not to wonder if many refuse to embrace the Gospel; because no man will ever of himself be able to come to Christ, but God must first approach him by his Spirit; and hence it follows that all are not drawn, but that God bestows this grace on those whom he has elected. True, indeed, as to the kind of drawing, it is not violent, so as to compel men by external force; but still it is a powerful impulse of the Holy Spirit, which makes men willing who formerly were unwilling and reluctant.*[61]

P stands for Perseverance of the Saints. This would seem to be a given consequence whatever view of Grace we adopt. However, it must be borne in mind, that to Calvin, it means it is God who perseveres with us. God guarantees those whom he has irresistibly drawn he will keep. This is an obvious conclusion because as God is Sovereign, anyone who has believed cannot be allowed to fall away. 2 Timothy 2:10-13. This was all wrapped up on the absolute sovereignty of God, who made Grace effective through his irrevocable decrees.

Jacobus Arminius. 1560-1609.

The third reformer we must consider is **Jakob Hermanszoon** better known as Jacob Arminius.

Arminius was raised in The Netherlands. He became a priest and theologian. He was well educated but as he was born later, he received a much broader input from the various streams of the reformation than the narrow Calvin/Luther approach. Arminius, because he dared to contradict the mighty Calvin, was persecuted, vilified and mocked both during and after his lifetime down to the present day.

---

[61] Institutes of the Christian Religion. John Calvin

Arminius' followers, after his early death, developed 5 points to challenge Calvin.[62] It was known in Holland as the 'Remonstrant.' He taught human will is free and not predetermined. He taught Total Depravity in the sense that sin was universal and affected the whole of Adam's race. However, man was not so depraved that he could not respond to the call of Grace. The will of man still had to be enabled. But this was by the work of the Holy Spirit at the time, not a pre-Adamic decree. The enabling did not automatically indicate conversion would result.

He taught that the foreknowledge of God enabled him to know what any person would choose to do. God's choosing or predestining of people for salvation was based on this foreknowledge, not arbitrary choosing.

He taught that the Atonement of Christ was sufficient for all to be saved. However, he acknowledged that all would not be saved, because some would choose not to believe. God had foreseen those who would in fact believe, but he did not determine it. The Atonement was entirely a work of God, but the receiving of its benefits, was an act of the enabled human will.

He taught Grace was resistible. Mankind could reject God's Grace. Grace is not deterministic, that is, cause and effect, but it was an influence to produce a desired response. Rejection was the basis of eternal damnation and separation from God.

He taught that Perseverance was not only a work of God but contained human responsibilities. Arminius conceded only to the 'possibility' that a person who had once believed could renege on the commitment they had made and fall from

---

[62] Arminianism. Slife.org. et al

Grace. He firmly proclaimed the keeping power of God through the ongoing work of the Holy Spirit.

Arminius became involved because he was asked to study the subject relating to the supposed decrees that shaped Grace and produce a paper on his finding to settle a dispute. He was expected to come out in favour of the views of Calvin, but in fact he came out with quite opposite opinions.

This triggered in him a dissatisfaction with what had been made of Calvin's teachings. He was particularly and increasingly disturbed by the doctrines of limited atonement and irresistible Grace. He began to feel, writing some 30 years after Calvin's death, that Calvinism was becoming tyrannical. Indeed, both Calvin and Calvinism reflected a similar intolerance for opposition that the system they sought to dismantle had done. Slowly Arminius moved away from Calvinism and his followers produced the teachings we now know as Arminianism

> *Arminius taught of a preventing (or prevenient) grace that has been conferred upon all by the Holy Spirit and this grace is 'sufficient for belief, in spite of our sinful corruption, and thus for salvation.' Arminius stated that the grace sufficient for salvation is conferred on the Elect, and on the non-Elect; that, if they will, they may believe or not believe, may be saved or not be saved.* [63]

Arminius was a much gentler soul than Calvin, by all accounts. He was much more tolerant of opposing views. He wrote of Calvin:

> *I encourage the reading of the commentaries of Calvin, which I extol with the greatest praise...For I say that he is incomparable in the interpretation of Scripture, and his comments are better*

---

[63] Biography of Jacobus Arminius.

than anything which the Fathers give us.[64]

Obviously, this all implies that Arminius viewed the Sovereignty of God differently from Calvin and Luther, and leant a little in the direction of Pelagius. To oppose Calvin, one had to dismantle what he meant by his basic premise, God's Supreme Sovereignty, controlling every aspect of life.

The Five *Solae.*

The five great pillars of evangelical faith that arose from the works of the Reformers have been complied by later reviewers of their writings. The reformers did not categorise their beliefs to this extent but the points are observable in an unconnected way in their writings. It can be seen that the purpose of these declarations was to affirm that no part of mankind's salvation was as a result of any human effort. It was something that exists only at God's initiative.

Sola Gratia. By Grace alone. The knowledge of sins forgiven and the promise of eternal life was a state brought about only by the fact God desired to do so to benefit the state fallen man.

Sola Fide. By Faith alone. Entrance into the state of Grace was only by believing the promises God had made. This faith was also a gift from God enabling the sinner to believe.

Sola Scriptura. From the scriptures alone. The evidence the sinner was asked to believe was what was contained in the word of God only and not the traditions of the church.

Solus Christus. By Christ alone. The act of removing the inherited sin of Adam, and the forgiveness of personal sin was only possible through the atonement Christ offered through

---

[64] Jacobus Arminius to Sebastian Egbert. 1607.

his own death and resurrection.

Soli Deo Gloria. For the Glory of God alone. The whole process of salvation and the benefits of the gospel were not primarily for the relief of mankind's predicament. They were first and foremost to declare God's Glory. This was done by showing how he could remove the guilt and power of sin and how he could punish those who persisted in wickedness.

These statements are the finest framework of the gospel of Grace ever written. They are the triumph of the dedication of the reformers over the state of affairs they were called to deal with. This is our legacy. This is the solid rock on which we must forever stand.

The Grace Space

CHAPTER SIX

Reflections

This is where the Reformation brought us to and left us, for 500 years. It was ignited by a religion of fear and self-deprecation. A Church focused on its own self-grandeur. Christian believers were utterly depraved but would hopefully find a place in God's heaven. They needed to correctly navigate their way through the minefield of venial and mortal sins. They needed to observe the rituals of baptism, confession, penance, and face the dreaded purgatory, scavenging morsels of Grace along the way. Until with much trepidation they would just about make it to their eternal reward, with some merit transferred from the saints to help along the way.

It ended with a clear Gospel of certainty. Sins were forgiven by faith in the work of Christ. No human effort was required, there was nothing to pay, nothing to do except believe, Christ had done it all. Eternity was secure and nothing could divert the believer from his destiny. Nothing could undo the state of Grace of a believer once entered into. Sadly however, this only applied to the elite few whom God had decreed would receive it, the remainder of humanity would face eternal hell. It was as it turned out, an 'Arrested Reformation.' [65]

The first Christians believed that Grace was available to all by the act of repentance and confession of the individual and thereby forged a personal relationship with God through Jesus Christ. This had changed by the 4th century by demonstrating that Grace was available to all, in good standing with the church, through participation in the sacraments as dispensed by the church.

As the Reformation settled down the predominant view was that Grace was freely available through faith. This experience of Grace was irrevocable and was not obtained or maintained by any human effort. But it was only available to those whom God had chosen to receive it. It was this that galvanised Arminius into action.

The views devised by Calvin and edited by his successors became the dominant view in protestant churches for the foreseeable future. I would like to ask why it was that Calvinism gained the upper hand when really its central message was austere and melancholic? After all Calvin's gospel amounted to the fact that all mankind was totally depraved with no hope of salvation or avoiding eternal hell, unless by sheer chance, God had placed their name in the list of Elect! But it did dominate. Why? I would suggest the following:

1. The Calvinist Reformers had control of many printing presses and could publish their own literature and their own Bible, the Geneva Bible, in unheard of quantities for the time.

2. The Calvinist Reformers offered a gospel that was austere but certain, exclusive but secure, and which comprehensively brought order to all areas of living. In the

---

[65] Dr David Allen. The Unfailing Stream

very 'class conscious' European world where the message was first proclaimed, it settled easily into the thinking of the day.

3. The Calvinist Reformers presented an intellectually satisfying explanation of the gospel, that as long as one accepted the propositions, it was an irrefutable argument. As well as satisfying 'deeper thinkers' this also appealed to the less privileged and educated. To claim they had grasped the reformed teaching, psychologically elevated their feelings of self-worth. They were now a part of God's chosen people.

4. The Reformation was a reformation of society as well as the church. If the government of the region in which one lived were followers of the Calvinist Reformers, it was pointless to oppose that if you wanted a quiet life.

5. It was an able riposte to Medieval Catholicism.

For quite some time Arminius and those who gave credence to his views, were forced into the outer orbit of Christian thought. Anti-Calvinist writings and expression were banned by law and it was not unknown for Arminians to be executed. Slowly, however, scholars arose in the Church of England that began to lean in favour of Arminius.

King James 1 (1602-1625) was strongly in favour of Calvin and consequently so was the Church in England. Charles 1 favoured the Arminianist views because they favoured the Divine Right of Kings. However, after the execution of Charles 1 (1625-1649) the Calvinists ruled through the republic of Oliver Cromwell. With the restoration of the monarchy in 1660, Charles 2, being more inclined to Catholicism, was also more inclined to Arminianism. Hence, the king being head of the church, the church followed his ideas. We can trace the matter through the next centuries but it would digress from the subject of this book. Suffice it to say Arminianism and its derivatives gained more and more traction in the English state church as time went by.

However, it was the ministry of John Wesley (1703-1791) and his brother Charles (1707-1788) that gave the Arminian position the popularity which has persisted to the present time. Even Charles Spurgeon (1834-1892), an ardent Calvinist, salutes the enthusiasm and passion of Wesley, if not his doctrine. The renowned 20th century evangelist, Billy Graham, was more inspired by Wesley than anyone else.

> *Doctor J. Edwin Orr, the greatest authority ever on revival in the church was a lecturer at Wheaton College. He took some students in 1940 in a brief visit to England, to visit the Epworth refectory where John Wesley was based. Beside the bed are two worn impressions in the carpet where it was said that John Wesley knelt for hours in prayer for England's social and spiritual renewal. As the students were getting on the bus, he noticed one missing. Going back upstairs, he found one student kneeling in the carpet kneeholes praying with his face on the bed. "Oh Lord, do it again! Do it again!" Orr placed a hand on the student's shoulder and said gently, "Come on Billy, we must be going." And rising, Billy Graham joined the bus.*

Like Calvin the successors of Arminius made more of his teachings than he did and so the position has many shades of meaning, some reaching in the reformed direction, some reaching towards Pelagius.

In my opinion, Arminius made a massive contribution to our understanding of Grace despite the severe persecution he suffered. Whether or not he was totally right in his conclusions is not the point. What matters is that his contribution enables us to move back to an understanding of Grace more in line with the first believers than what Calvinism, left to its own devices, would have enabled us to do.

Roots and fruits.

We are quite well aware of the famous saying of Jesus when he said,

> *Every good tree bears good fruit, and every bad tree bad fruit.* Matthew 7:17

Certain fruit began to appear on the branches of Reformed Christianity from the 18th Century, which reflect to my mind something of the nature of the root. Certainly, a Calvinist philosophy raised little objection to American revivalists such as, Timothy Dwight Senior, Jonathan Edwards Senior and George Whitfield, to owning slaves.

The Reformed churches were nearer the heart of the problem in Northern Ireland than the heart of the solution for decades.

And in South Africa, the doctrine of Apartheid was not conceived in the chambers of parliament but in the synods of the Reformed Church. Thankfully things have moved on in more recent years.

I am not saying that other views produced a perfect world. They did not. Each had its *Achilles heel*. However, it did seem to be largely, but not totally, the case that the closer one was to Pelagianism the more likely you were to be involved in social reform, and the closer one was to Augustine, the less so. I can only assume that the root of this lay in the concept of a `*Limited Atonement.*' In fairness I must add, the Calvinist Charles Spurgeon was very much involved in social reform.

Things have changed dramatically, yet some things are more persistent. There seems to be an arrogance and intolerance detectable in the plethora of writings available. Many decry a gospel that appeals to, or persuades, the sinner to be saved. They baulk at the idea of a `sinner's prayer.' They are horrified of making a church 'seeker sensitive.' They claim that any aids to conversion, such as the Alpha programme, are acts of self-righteousness and are without merit before God.

Some years ago, while pondering on the matter of reaching people for Jesus, a picture came to my mind. I saw as it were, a church on a hill surrounded by a plain. There was a staircase that rose from the plain to the church and people making their way backwards and forwards. Then I saw that every now and again the plain would flood. Each time it flooded a little bit of the soil was washed away. This carried on year after year until the gap between the bottom step and the plain was so huge no one could climb it any more. Then the Lord seemed to say to me, "build more steps."

It seems to me Calvinism requires people to make a gigantic leap into Grace, so gigantic few can make it. Build more steps, not to make salvation easy, but to make it possible for a more depraved world to hear the gospel. After all, Calvin's converts were already 'Christian.' They had a fundamental, although distorted, knowledge of the Gospel and every aspect of their lives was regulated by religion. They were also part of the concept of the Elect, because that was the basis on which they moved to the 'New Religion.'

Two things are different today. Our unbelieving populations know absolutely nothing about God, the Bible and the work of Christ, not even in a sacramental way.

And I do not hold to 'generational salvation.' Hence as a rule I did not baptise babies, but dedicated them, and then nurture them, until they make their own decision to follow Jesus. The gap between Grace and sin is vast. We do not lower Grace and we do not build up sin. We simply build more steps. Those steps are stages whereby we can make Jesus known to a dying world by meeting people where they are, not where we would like them to be!

These are not steps of self-righteousness, it is rather:

> *The mind that was in Christ Jesus when he humbled himself to the death of the cross.'* Philippians 2: 5-7.

An intellectual intolerance.

Calvin himself was intolerant of views at variance to his own. He advocated that the jurisdiction of Geneva didn't tolerate Christian expressions different to his own, both in secular and ecclesiastical government. To his eternal chagrin he was complicit in the execution of one, Miguel Serveto, deemed as a heretic and incinerated in flames produced from the burning of his own books. [66] In my own experience there remains, in reading countless articles for this chapter, a certain arrogance in Calvinistic writers, un-called for in the handling of Holy Scripture.

I am amazed to find that when Calvin was asked to describe his conversion experience, there was nothing I could find about brokenness in guilt and shame at the foot of the cross; no being overwhelmed by the substitutionary suffering; no expression of love and adoration for the One who died; and no tears of repentance or joy of sins forgiven. All that he could say was,'

> *At first, although I was so obstinately given to the superstitions of the papacy, that it was extremely difficult to drag me from the depths of the mire, yet by a sudden conversion He tamed my heart and made it teachable, this heart which for its age was excessively hardened in such matters.* [67]

It was otherwise translated as;

---

[66] Encyclopaedia Brittanica
[67] The Conversion of Calvin. irp-cdn.multiscreensite.com/.

By a sudden conversion, God subdued and brought my heart to docility. [68]

I do not doubt the sincerity of Calvin's conversion. He describes at length the battle to turn his back on the form of religion he had known from birth and of which he was persuaded it was his only hope of salvation. He describes the liberty he found from his search of the scriptures. Yet the overall tone intimates the fact it was fundamentally an intellectual experience. We can see that the observable fruit is consistent with the nature of the root.

I would endorse the description of salvation by Calvinists, that it is a moment of 'enlightenment,' a spiritual experience, un-aided by anyone. The person is made aware of their depravity and their need of God's Grace, and faith wells up within them in order that they begin to believe.

But I cannot demote the validity of the experience of the person who believes as a result of having the gospel explained to them and prays a prayer of commitment. It is arrogant to say that there is no 'enlightenment' of the Holy Spirit in regard to the horror of sin and the goodness of Grace in such an encounter.

It is also arrogant to say that only the former reflects Gods sovereign choice to save the individual. How can we prescribe what took place in one realm, eternity, and how that should be worked out in time? Is not the apparent 'Calvinist' conversion of Paul and the more 'Arminian' conversion of Apollos (Acts 18: 24-28) equally authentic?

---

[68] M H Watts. The importance of Calvin Today.

Duplicity

Preachers of a Calvinistic persuasion will accept that it is their duty to preach the gospel to whoever will listen. But only the Elect will respond. They will have to do this because they do not know who the Elect are. In this they give the impression that the gospel is equitable and available to all, but in fact it is not. They cannot truly say to the congregation, '*Jesus died for you,*' because there could well be one, or indeed many, present, whom Jesus did not die for!

What is the point of telling a congregation they are totally depraved and then saying there is nothing they can do about it? Or telling them there is a salvation for the elect but there is no way of knowing if they are among that number. Even the greatest of preachers, the noble Charles Spurgeon battled here.

> *Lord, hasten to bring in all Thine elect—and then elect some more.*[69]

I accept that the statement, in its context, can be taken as 'tongue in cheek,' but it indicates, the great man, although an ardent follower of Calvin, longed for some latitude in its strictures. He makes no attempt to reconcile such a statement with the doctrine, although I cannot doubt, he understood the implications only too well.

The matter also involves baptism. Most reformed churches follow Calvin in paedo-baptism. It is believed the baptism of the children of believing parents is a sign and seal of their salvation. All that is now required is to be instructed in the faith and to remain in the faith and they are 'saved.' No further conversion experience is required. This is duplicitous because it makes the initial step of salvation an act of the faith of

---

[69] W Y Fullerton. Biography of Spurgeon. Chapter 8.

others. Such a process can result in the sound and secure conversion of the individual, because God is sovereign and can work in spite of any system. But the system itself gives a false assurance.

The author of sin.

The Reformed position vehemently denies that God is the author of sin. However, the position of absolute sovereignty makes this difficult to explain.

To quote *Grace.org* again;

> *What about sin? God is not the author of sin, but He certainly allowed it; it is integral to His eternal decree. God has a purpose for allowing it. He cannot be blamed for evil or tainted by its existence 1 Sam. 2:2: There is no one holy like the Lord. But He certainly wasn't caught off-guard or standing helpless to stop it when sin entered the universe. We do not know His purpose for allowing sin. Clearly, in the general sense, He allowed sin in order to display His glory— attributes that would not be revealed apart from evil— mercy, grace, compassion, forgiveness, and salvation. And God sometimes uses evil to accomplish good Gen. 45:7– 8; 50:20; Rom. 8:28. How can these things be? Scripture does not answer all the questions, but it does teach that God is utterly sovereign, perfectly holy, and absolutely just.*

Either evil and righteousness both originate with God, or righteousness originates with God and evil comes from another source.

As God is sovereign, evil can only arise if God permits it, or if God creates creatures with such autonomy that they can devise evil within themselves apart from God. The purpose of such autonomous beings would be *sola deo Gloria* but not because they were programmed to do so, but they did so from the motivation of their own autonomous free will. I intend to show that I believe this is the best explanation.

God does not require evil through which to display his glory. In fact, God does not require anything in creation to show his glory, his glory exists for its own sake.

Jesus spoke of the Glory of God, which was to be the destiny of his followers, as being the same Glory that was enjoyed before the creation of the world. The Glory, that is the grace, mercy, love and kindness of God, was evident before man sinned.

> *For the very glory you have given to me I have given them so that they will be joined together as one and experience the same unity that we enjoy. You live fully in me and now I live fully in the so that they will experience perfect unity, and the world will be convinced that you have sent me, for they will see that you love each one of them with the same passionate love that you have for me. "Father, I ask that you allow everyone that you have given to me to be with me where I am! Then they will see my full glory— the very splendour you have placed upon me because you have loved me even before the beginning of time.* John 17:22-24. Passion translation.

Paul also tells us that the depravity of man is devoid of the glory of God.

> *Because, although they knew God, they did not glorify Him as God, nor were thankful, but became futile in their thoughts, and their foolish hearts were darkened. Professing to be wise, they became fools, and changed the glory of the incorruptible God into an image made like corruptible man—and birds and four-footed animals and creeping things.* Romans 1: 21-23.

If God made a decree to permit evil, how is it then claimed that all those who do not believe are justly condemned? Yet the reason they do not believe is that God has refused to enable them to do so.

It is further problematic in the case if someone believes and then reneged on their belief, it is said that they received Grace for salvation but not for perseverance. This means that God allowed an obstacle to be placed in their path which he knew they would not be able to overcome. So, breaking the promise in 1 Corinthians 10:13 and making nonsense of 2 Timothy 1:12. He evidently was not able to keep that which had been committed onto him!

Human experience.

Human society is so organised to repress the wanton and rampant expression of human will. Wherever mankind lives in a community there has to regulations. Why is this so? Why is it that creatures like us who were designed to live together find it so hard to do so?

It is because everyone's will *is* intrinsically free, and without regulation, there would be chaos. Calvinism, no matter how it arranges its wording, has to accept that its method of salvation comes about by an irresistible inevitability. This need, to subject the will presupposes the autonomy of the will in the first place.

The final word?

Reformed doctrine comes to us today enforced by '*The Westminster Confession* 1646,' and the '*Canons of Dortrecht*.' 1618' The former became the foundational document for the Reformation in Great Britain and the later was meant to silence Arminius in favour of Calvin in Europe. It seems to me, from Calvin's own words and the comments of his successors that it was believed they had devised something that was the 'final word' on Christian Doctrine. It was futile to contradict it because in theological terms this was '*the theory of everything.'*

Human experience has taught us that to claim such a monopoly on knowledge should set alarm bells ringing.

If a man stands in an expansive plateau two things can be concluded from what he sees. The earth is flat and saucer shaped, and the sun orbits the earth, and for centuries everyone was happy with that. Neither of these observations of course are true. It is only when we observe the earth in relation to the universe, we see what is actually the case. Since this was established as the fact of the matter, it has dawned upon us that we will never know everything. We will never come to the point in this life where there is nothing else to discover.

The Reformed view claims it has harmonised all scripture into one interpretation. I don't think so. It has harmonised some scriptures, re-interpreted some, and banished others to the outer orbit of useful knowledge. *Every commentator, including me, has done the same.* It depends on the starting point. Start where Calvin started you will end where Calvin ends! Starting with a different understanding of Divine Sovereignty, one can reach different conclusions.

The crucial difference is that what I have said leaves loose ends, *'known-unknowns and unknown-unknowns'* if you like. It does not claim to answer everything because everything cannot be explained from the scriptures we have. They were written that way so that we will never be able to come to that place when we are capable of knowing all.

Ben Witherington, commenting on an interview with John Piper, writes about the New Testament authors;

> *Their faith in God is not based on a conviction that they have a coherent theological system which they in essence*

fully understand and can explain. Their faith in God comes from having a personal relationship with God which provided them with enough evidence to produce faith in God. They know enough to know-- that they don't know enough to produce a comprehensive system called 'the knowledge of God.

T S Elliot wrote in his poem, The Waste Land, these apt words:

All our knowledge brings us nearer to our ignorance, All our ignorance brings us nearer to death, but nearness to death no nearer to God. Where is the life we have lost in living? Where is the wisdom we have lost in knowledge? Where is the knowledge we have lost in information?

Paul writing to Timothy about the nature of the scriptures says the following:

And that from childhood you have known the Holy Scriptures, which are able to make you wise for salvation through faith which is in Christ Jesus. All Scripture is given by inspiration of God, and is profitable for doctrine, for reproof, for correction, for instruction righteousness, that the man of God may be complete, thoroughly equipped for every good work. 2 Timothy 3:15-17.

The scriptures are sufficient to bring to faith and keep us there but they are not a comprehensive knowledge of God.

For now we see in a mirror, dimly, but then face to face. Now I know in part, but then I shall know just as I also am known. 1 Corinthians 13:12.

The standard Reformed position contains much wonderful revelation, but I fear, that the glue that holds it together has been merged with the revelation to the point one can no longer see the difference.

How it is that some believe and some do not, and God was able to see that millions of years ago, is an utter mystery. However, everyone that has come to believe has co-operated with a gift of faith that God has deposited in their heart. Everyone who has not come to believe has somehow resisted and negated that gift of faith to the point it is rendered ineffective. There are experiences of grace that are beyond the imagination of all the Reformers. They made a giant leap forward in the understanding and application of scripture, but what they left us with, I dare to say, is by no means, '*The Final Word.*'

The Grace Space

CHAPTER SEVEN

Another look at God's sovereignty

I think the foregoing brief historical survey is sufficient for us to understand where we are today. The next four chapters reflect my convictions on the matter and are based on what I believe to be a fairer interpretation of scripture.

Catholicism and Orthodoxy did not go away, but the stranglehold on the spiritual destiny of people was forever broken. We have also come to realise that people can stand firmly and securely in the Grace of God and yet visibly be part of any of the Christian Communities. As the Reformation settled into normal church life, the two dominant views on Grace were adopted by various protestant streams. Of course, there are variants but what was dubbed Calvinism and Arminianism remain the two principal schools of thought to the present day.

We can now analyse these conclusions, not hounded, as was Augustine, by Pelagius, or haunted by the corruption, and threatened with the power of the Roman Church, as were Luther and Calvin. We can reflect at a more leisurely pace and align what we believe with the scriptures without the encumbrance of philosophy. After all, we have more to take into consideration than Calvin did. His determinism [70] was well and good for the 16th century, but Calvin did not have to reconcile the absolute will of God with the Enlightenment, the Slave Trade, the Holocaust, and even Covid. Neither did he need to find a place for his austere understanding of God with modern expressions of Christianity.

I find a paucity in Calvin of the use of the concepts of Mercy, Compassion, Love and Kindness when it comes to the character of God. If the first flourishing of his views is evidenced in those we have called '*The Puritans*' then I don't think these observations are far from the truth. They left a legacy of a somewhat impassioned and austere religion. Such descriptions of Grace leave us uncomfortable today. Well, they leave me as uncomfortable, as Luther also firstly confessed. Unlike Luther, who then was able to juxtapose his thoughts so that he saw '*health in the intolerable*,' I remain uncomfortable. It sounds so ruthless, clinical and heartless. The sad thing was, as it turned out, it was just that.

> There was a coldness and hardness about Calvin's mind, which led him sometimes to regard as objects of mere intellect, those things which could not but deeply move the feelings of minds differently constituted; and hence, I cannot but concur, he did not duly appreciate the effect of the language that he was using upon other persons. And to these extreme statements and this obnoxious language, I must think, is to be traced to a considerable portion of that storm of obloquy and odium which has not ceased to beat

---

[70] That is everything is a result of Divine Decrees.

upon the head of Calvin and Calvinism to this day.[71]

I write from the age in which I live. Today we regard emotion as an authentic expression of the soul. We can be sombre in church, but we can also laugh, cry and show our feelings. We see a God who can also laugh, cry, love and care. It is not weakness but reality.

Calvin's system of theology, given the assumption of the absolute Sovereignty of God, is logically watertight and irrefutable. As such it became a suitable framework for an alternative to the 'Old Faith.' But we must ask, is it to be the foundational view of Grace for all time?

'Another look' is to see what we have discovered about God in the 400 years since the Reformation. We must start where Calvin started and dare to ask, is Calvin's conception of Divine Sovereignty correct? I am fully aware, that even today, to question Calvin, is seen as a form of heresy in some circles.

Many today would claim to hold Calvin's views on Grace but deny that Jesus only died for the Elect, or that some people were born to be damned. The need to modify what has been made of Calvin, by professing Calvinists, indicates to me that I am not alone in my feelings of discomfort. They identify themselves as 3 or 4, or even as the highly esteemed R.T. Kendall does, a 4½ point Calvinist! [72]

However, I would contend that the five points of '*TULIP*' attributed to Calvin and presented today as Reformed Doctrine are interdependent and to remove or modify one, causes them all to fall.

---

[71] History of Protestantism. Scott.

[72] R T Kendall ministries. Online. The points in question are the 5 points of the TULIP acronym.

> *Sometimes people will say they are a three-point Calvinist or a four-point Calvinist, but this cannot be so. Calvinism as a whole cannot be broken down into separate parts just because that person doesn't feel that he or she cannot cope with a certain perspective. Three, and four-point Calvinists, are simply confused Arminians.* [73]

To say, as Kendall does, that Jesus died for all, but only interceded for the elect, amounts to the same thing. I cannot see how it can be avoided, to believe that God determined an Elect must also determine that there exists a 'non-Elect,' or reprobate, they cannot just be a people whom God ignored.

The Supreme Sovereignty of God.

The following quotation well reflects the Reformed view of sovereignty.

> *No doctrine is more despised by the natural mind than the truth that God is absolutely sovereign. Human pride loathes the suggestion that God orders everything, controls everything, and rules over everything. The carnal mind, burning with enmity against God, abhors the Biblical teaching that nothing comes to pass except according to His eternal decrees. Most of all, flesh hates the notion that salvation is entirely God's work. If God chose who would be saved, and if His choice was settled before the foundation of the world, then believers deserve no credit for any aspect of their salvation.* [74]

Surely Calvin and the Church Fathers are right here? God knows everything past, present and future and has decreed all that will happen both good and evil. Nothing can happen without his will. His word will never fail. Such understanding lies at the heart of assurance, confidence and faith in God.

---

[73] Dr. Matthew McMahon

[74] Grace.org.

That they may know from the rising of the sun to its setting That there is none besides Me. I am the Lord, and there is no other; I form the light and create darkness, I make peace and create calamity; I, the Lord, do all these things. Rain down, you heavens, from above, and let the skies pour down righteousness; let the earth open, let them bring forth salvation, and let righteousness spring up together. I, the Lord, have created it. Woe to him who strives with his Maker!
Let the potsherd strive with the potsherds of the earth! Shall the clay say to him who forms it, what are you making? Or shall your handiwork say, He has no hands? Woe to him who says to his father, what are you begetting? Or to the woman, what have you brought forth? Isaiah 45:6-10.

Who is he who speaks and it comes to pass, when the Lord has not commanded it? Is it not from the mouth of the Most High that woe and well-being proceed? Why should a living man complain, a man for the punishment of his sins? Lamentations 3:36-39.

Yours, O Lord, is the greatness, the power and the glory, The victory and the majesty; for all that is in heaven and in earth is Yours; Yours is the kingdom, O Lord, and You are exalted as head over all. Both riches and honour come from You, and You reign over all. In Your hand is power and might; in Your hand it is to make great and to give strength to all. 1 Chronicles 29: 11-12.

I believe in the Absolute Sovereignty of God, as did all the Reformers, and is clearly portrayed in the plain text of the scriptures. But this is not the whole picture.

Devolved Sovereignty.

As we search through the pages of the scriptures, I believe I find in scripture another phenomenon. That is *Devolved Sovereignty*. I see in the scriptures a teaching that tells us that God has devolved certain levels of sovereignty to others, for example, a man in his family, a magistrate in society, a king in a country. [75] Furthermore, this devolution is not a matter of subordinates reiterating the will of the master, but they have been granted a true autonomy. Although they are expected to act righteously, they can act unrighteously. In either case they are responsible before God for the decisions they make. I cannot consent to the conclusion, that at any time, God said something like, *'Between 1933 and 1945, there will be, or even permit, a holocaust, just to display how holy I am and how sinful man is!'* We have to conclude God did not do this and that evil is a phenomenon that can arise out of devolved Sovereignty.

To Adam;

> *Then God said, 'Let Us make man in Our image, according to Our likeness;* **let them have dominion** *over the fish of the sea, over the birds of the air, and over the cattle, over all the earth and over every creeping thing that creeps on the earth.' So, God created man in His own image; in the image of God He created him; male and female He created them. Then God blessed them, and God said to them, 'Be fruitful and multiply; fill the earth and* **subdue it; have dominion** *over the fish of the sea, over the birds of the air, and over every living thing that moves on the earth.'* Genesis 1:26-28.

In regard to earthly authorities;

> *Jesus answered, you could have no power at all against Me unless it had been given you from above. Therefore, the one who delivered Me to you has the greater sin.* John 19:11.

Pilate has said that he has the power to release or condemn

---

[75] The Institute of Basic life principles.

Jesus. Jesus does not dispute that but points out that the power is devolved from God. As a result, he should be very careful how he uses his power.

> Therefore, **submit yourselves to every ordinance of man** for the Lord's sake, whether to the king as supreme, or to governors, as to **those who are sent by him** for the punishment of evildoers and for the praise of those who do good. For this is the will of God, that by doing good you may put to silence the ignorance of foolish men—as free, yet not using liberty as a cloak for vice, but as bondservants of God. Honour all people. Love the brotherhood. Fear God. **Honour the king.** 1 Peter 2:13-17

> Therefore, whoever resists the authority **resists the ordinance of God,** and those who resist will bring judgment on themselves. For rulers are not a terror to good works, but to evil. Do you want to be unafraid of the authority? Do what is good, and you will have praise from the same. For he is God's minister to you for good. But if you do evil, be afraid; for he does not bear the sword in vain; **for he is God's minister, an avenger to execute wrath on him who practices evil.** Therefore, you must be subject, not only because of wrath but also for conscience' sake. For because of this you also pay taxes, for they are **God's ministers** attending continually to this very thing. Render therefore to all their due: taxes to whom taxes are due, customs to whom customs, fear to whom fear, honour to whom honour. Romans 13; 2-7

In relation to Church Leaders:

> The elders who are among you I exhort, I who am a fellow elder and a witness of the sufferings of Christ, and also a partaker of the glory that will be revealed: Shepherd the flock of God which is among you, serving as **overseers,** not by compulsion but willingly, not for dishonest gain but eagerly; nor as being lords over those entrusted to you,

but being examples to the flock; and when the Chief Shepherd appears, you will receive the crown of glory that does not fade away. 1 Peter 5:1-4.

The principle continued; within the family. Ephesians 6:1-4; Colossians 3: 18-21. Again, this shows us that there is devolved authority, but not without accountability.

Gods gives such people limited sovereignty in their spheres of operation. He also gives them strict parameters by which they are to carry out their responsibilities. The gift of autonomous free-will is to be regarded as a treasured gift of God, bestowed under God's Sovereign authority, designed to bring glory to God. It is a privilege not a right! There are things they are expected to do. And he will hold all to account for the way they have exercised their sovereignty on the day of judgement.

Surely the parable of the Stewards in Matthew 25: 14-30, illustrates the principles of Devolved Sovereignty. The stewards were given an amount of money each, to invest as they saw fit. They each acted independently and autonomously but they would be required to give an account of what they had done, and would be judged accordingly. The judgement was entirely on the merits of what each of the stewards had done, or not done. They were accountable for their actions irrespective of the amount they received.

God remains ultimately Sovereign. He can overrule as He pleases. The devolution is part of His sovereignty. It does not take away from it. Although we live under the devolved authority of other men and women, we are to execute our tasks as if we were working directly for God. Colossians 3:17. However, it is obvious that there are people who have attained a place of authority who rule without consideration of the will of God.

This brings me to the understanding that sometimes things will happen that God will know about beforehand because he sees what is in the heart of man. But he did not plan, execute, or permit these things. Only in the sense he had devolved the authority so making it possible for such decisions to be made, can the acts of men be linked to God.

God will override the decisions of people to bring about his purposes in the matter of the outworking of world redemption. That is in everything to do with the first and second coming of Jesus Christ. Life experience will indicate that the decisions of people are authentic and autonomous. As is evident in the fact that God usually intervenes with redemption in the aftermath, rather than prevention in the first place.

I believe the Sovereignty of God is far greater than what is now presented as Calvinism. In Calvinism, Gods Sovereignty is established by the removal of any realistic opposition. God determines all that happens. Whatever is done, good or evil, is the will of God. The presence of sin and evil is explained by the claim that the evil perpetrated also glorifies God in the manifestation of his righteous judgements. Holiness is magnified by the background of sin. In fact, what has been made of Calvinism implies that evil and the people who perpetrate it were decreed into existence just so God could confine them to eternal hell.

I see the Sovereignty of God in that mankind can make certain free and independent decisions of its own volition, but God is able to redeem any course of action man has taken. Joseph was well aware of this when he was reconciled with his brothers.

Do not be afraid, for am I in the place of God? But as for you, you intended evil against me, but God meant it for good in order to bring it about as it is today, to save many people. Genesis 50:19-20.

I would contend that the act of Joseph's brothers was not determined by God, it was their decision. Their evil intent was fulfilled for a while. It may well have been God's intention to bring Joseph to Egypt, but by other means. Certainly, there are some things that God has declared will happen, and will see to it that they do. But not all things. In this we see another dimension of his sovereignty. He will bring to pass the things he has specifically determined, even though man will make free decisions along the way. No one will ever act beyond God's Sovereignty, but within certain parameters man can rebel against God.

We cannot say that the devolved authority exercised by men and women was determined by God in every case. The decisions taken were volitional and autonomous, but the individuals are accountable to God for what they have done with the responsibility they were given.

God's sovereignty will continue to be shared with his people in the age to come, because we will be joint-heirs with Christ (Romans 8; 17) and reign with him. (2 Timothy 2:12)

Alternate History.

Not only can God see the decisions that will be made, he can see the options that were assessed and rejected in any decision-making process. At any crossroads God can see all the possible roads ahead. (Psalm 139: 1-6) There is always the right choice, and varying options until you get to the catastrophic choice. Although it matters which road is taken, God is entirely capable of placing a redeeming situation along any of the possible pathways. In this way God is sovereign and human choice is autonomous. Mankind is capable of rejecting God's redeeming interventions and proceed along his chosen path. Such a course of action will eventually end in judgement.

God's sovereignty takes into consideration alternate history. It covers the matter of options. Whichever option a person takes, God is able to turn the repercussions of that decision to his glory.

> *The lot is cast into the lap, but its every decision is from the Lord.* Proverbs 16:33

God laid before Cain alternatives.

> *If you do the right thing, you will be accepted. If you do not do the right thing, then sin lies at the door.....what have you done?.....so from now on......* Genesis 4:6-14.

God was saying to Cain, I will be in both options. One way you will find redemption through blessing, and the other you may find redemption through correction. I will bring about my plan with mankind whatever you choose to do, you may or may not be part of it. Depending on what you choose, I will have to take different actions to accomplish it. God could see the course of both options.

Mordecai laid before Esther, alternatives.

> *And Mordecai told them to answer Esther: "Do not think in your heart that you will escape in the king's palace any more than all the other Jews. For if you remain completely silent at this time, relief and deliverance will arise for the Jews from another place, but you and your father's house will perish. Yet who knows whether you have come to the kingdom for such a time as this?* Esther 4:13-14.

The scriptures are saying here the deliverance would come to the Jewish people without any doubt. Whether it would be through Esther or someone else was not of paramount importance. God would bring it about through whoever was willing to speak out.

Elisha gave options to Joash:

> *And he said, 'Open the east window; and he opened it. Then Elisha said, Shoot; and he shot. And he said, "The arrow of the Lord's deliverance and the arrow of deliverance from Syria; for you must strike the Syrians at Aphek till you have destroyed them." Then he said, Take the arrows, so, he took them. And he said to the king of Israel, Strike the ground; so, he struck three times, and stopped. And the man of God was angry with him, and said, you should have struck five or six times; then you would have struck Syria till you had destroyed it! But now you will strike Syria only three times."* 2 Kings 13:17-19.

We must assume the future would have been different if his action had been different. Either option was open to him. God would be in the options, but the one would have been better than the other.

There is the episode of David and the angel of Judgment. 1 Chronicles 21:10-15. David was given three options from the Lord. He chose one of them, and that was the course of history.

Are we to suppose that when God places options before people it is like an actor responding to a pre-planned cue on the stage, or are they genuine volitional acts of the will?

Whichever option David had chosen, the Lord would have brought redemption somewhere along the road. Although the journey would have been very different in each case.

There is another amazing statement in Matthew 26:53.

> *But Jesus said to him, "Put your sword in its place, for all who take the sword will perish by the sword. Or do you think*

that I cannot now pray to My Father, and He will provide Me with more than twelve legions of angels? How then could the Scriptures be fulfilled, that it must happen thus?"

Jesus had just prayed;

"If it is possible let this cup pass from me, but nevertheless not as I will, but as you will." Matthew 26:39.

As for our Lord, his destiny was the cross. What a conflict! Yet here two alternatives suddenly present themselves, either of which, although possible, would have contradicted the scriptures. Peter's option was to go to war now. Jesus' own option was to call on the Father's standby, plan 'B,' legions of angels. It would have been the final judgement there and then. All redemption hung in the balance for a moment. It could have been only those who had believed up to that point, but our Lord embraced the cross.

Are the phrases, 'I have decided, I have made up my mind, I have chosen, and the *I Will* couples exchange at the altar,' all meaningless redundancies of speech? Or do they reflect the meaning they contain without being laundered through a philosophical mangle.

The word of God instructs believers to seek Gods will before making decisions, either through prayer Romans 12:2; wise counsel Proverbs 15:22; or from the scriptures, 1 Corinthians 10:1-13. It seems to me, if we are instructed to invoke Divine Guidance in our decision making, then our decisions are truly autonomous and will affect us, and others, for good or evil, so they need to made with caution. Repeatedly in scripture God asks people to choose. Deuteronomy 13:9; Joshua 24:15; 1 Samuel 8:18; 1 Kings 18:21. Surely such plain-speak means that the people in question truly made autonomous decisions.

Prayers of Supplication.

Jesus prayed prayers requesting for the course of history to change. He said about Peter, '*Satan has desired to sift you as wheat, but I have prayed for you.*' Luke 22: 31-32. In John 17 Jesus prays for the disciples, verses 11; 15; 20. Surely, these were genuine prayers for the change of a course, or the maintaining of a course in the face of a threat to disrupt the purposes of God. We must suppose that had the prayers not been made, the outcome would have been detrimentally different. It must indicate that even in matters to do with salvation and perseverance, things are not pre-programmed.

We must apply this to the prayers that we are encouraged to pray. '*We have not because we do not ask.*' James 4:2; John 16:24. We can ask, what is the point of praying, '*Thy will be done on earth as it is in heaven,*' if his will was going to be done on earth anyway? The prayer must pre-suppose that '*other wills*' were taking place on earth.

We must conclude that the magnificence of his Grace, the extent of his Sovereignty, and the power of his Love, is able to take, not only what he has determined, but what others have been permitted to determine by their own free will, and in the end bring all things to the Glory of His Name.

Having said this we must, at this point, bow our heads in humility. Exactly at what point the Divine Will and human autonomy meet is shrouded in mystery and we have to admit that the secret things belong to the Lord and there is a pathway we will never know. I have concluded that the philosophical process employed by Augustine and absorbed by Calvin and his redactors, have been attempts of human wisdom, to unravel the unsearchable wisdom of God.

For the message of the cross is foolishness to those who are perishing, but to us who are being saved it is the power of God. For it is written: "I will destroy the wisdom of the wise, and bring to nothing the understanding of the prudent." Where is the wise? Where is the scribe. Where is the disputer of this age? Has not God made foolish the wisdom of this world? For since, in the wisdom of God, the world through wisdom did not know God, it pleased God through the foolishness of the message preached to save those who believe. 1 Corinthians 1:18-21.

Grace is a space created entirely by God, with sin stacked up on one side and Divine judgment on the other, mankind is invited to enter by submission of their lives to the claims of the Gospel.

John 6: 44 remains true. No one comes to Jesus unless the Father draws them. But the 'drawing' is not the irresistible tug of a Divine bridle, but the inner working of the Holy Spirit of God in a person's life before they step into the Place of Grace. We must also point out that all those who are drawn do not stay. John 17: 12. Judas was one who was drawn, as Jesus explains,

> *And none of them perished except him whose nature it was to perish.*[76]

I don't think the '*son of perdition*' means Judas was individually selected to betray Jesus by God and had no choice. The '*son of perdition* ' was a role that had to be occupied because Jesus had to be betrayed. It could just as easily have been Peter. Matthew 16:23; Luke 22:31;

John 13:38; 18:10-11. Judas vacated his place of Grace. It remained for another to fill. Acts 1: 15-26. You may feel this was an error on behalf of the Apostles and that God was already preparing someone else for the role. Be that as it may,

---

[76] J C Ellicot quoting Luther.

the role of his apostleship did not fall away because Judas fell away. This was a prophetic fulfilment. Psalm 69:25; 109:8. If Judas had been decreed to betray, his apostleship would have perished with him, as there would have been no further role for him. Instead, his glorious calling continued by being given to another, while Judas perished because of the decisions he made.

To be made willing yet not to be forced, in my opinion, is playing with words. It just shifts the critical moment in the decision-making process. The working of the Holy Spirt makes known the option, but the decision is that of the person.

God acts in history.

The Bible records accounts of when God directly turned the course of history. The Flood, the Tower of Babel, and the coming of Jesus Christ are examples. It also indicates, that as we approach the end of this age, we can expect God to directly intervene in the course of history again.

God does not usually act directly in history. More often he manipulates natural phenomena in such a way that mankind makes decisions that bring about his purpose. At other times however, God allowed history to take its course and did not intervene. He allows evil to fully ripen. Instead, he provided Grace sufficient for the faithful to overcome the situations in which they found themselves.

> *For their heart was not steadfast with Him, nor were they faithful in His covenant. But He, being full of compassion, forgave their iniquity, and did not destroy them. Yes, many a time He turned His anger away, and did not stir up all His wrath; For He remembered that they were but flesh, a breath that passes away and does not come again.* Psalm 78; 37-39.

My view on Divine Sovereignty moves away from Calvin, Luther, and Arminius for that matter. God can determine to do whatever he pleases. But one of the things he has determined to do is to grant devolved and limited sovereignty to the descendants of Adam. Mankind may do things according to God's will, and bring glory to God. Man may also choose to do things against God's will. But even in those things God is still able to redeem the situation that ensues. We have been endowed with a priceless gift, free will, let us make sure that we use it for the purpose it was intended, to Glorify God and him alone.

The Grace Space

CHAPTER EIGHT

A fresh look at total depravity.

This aspect of the Doctrine of Grace was developed because it was felt essential that people understood there was no effort on their part that could persuade God to save them and there was nothing they could do to contribute to their salvation. They were not able so much as to choose to believe without the enabling of God. It was entirely a work of God. It was necessary to counter the state of affairs in the church at the time which was essentially 'Pelagianism', a doctrine of works.

Reformed writers often seem to include the qualifying phrase in their writings. '*This does not mean that man is as bad as he could be.*' If that is the case, I wonder why are the words '*total and utter,*' used? I would suggest it belies the motivation behind the doctrine, that has more to do with negating Pelagius than it does expounding the scriptures. I have difficulty in following Calvin here. It is in the concept that *Total*

Depravity equates to *Total Inability,* and to concede *Limited Ability* is to declare a salvation through *Self-Righteousness.*

I would propose the term, '*Universal Depravity,*' as the essential component of the Doctrine of Grace. There was something in the actions of Adam that affected the entire race and meant that everyone is born with a warp in their nature that determines by the time they understand good and evil they are already separated from God. It is ultimately a mystery but I don't see how it can be denied.

> *For all have sinned and fall short of the glory of God, being justified freely by his Grace through the Redemption that is in Jesus Christ.* Romans 3:23-24.

> *Therefore, just as through one man sin entered the world, and death through sin, and thus death spread to all men, because all sinned...... For if by the one man's offense death reigned through the one, much more those who receive abundance of grace and of the gift of righteousness will reign in life through the One, Jesus Christ.*
> *Therefore, as through one man's offense judgment came to all men, resulting in condemnation, even so through one Man's righteous act the free gift came to all men, resulting in justification of life. For as by one man's disobedience many were made sinners, so also by one Man's obedience many will be made righteous.* Romans 5:12-19.

> *But the natural man does not receive the things of the Spirit of God, for they are foolishness to him; nor can he know them, because they are spiritually discerned.* 1 Corinthians 2:14.

These and other scriptures clearly establish that '*all have sinned*' and stand in a state of sin before God. How the sin of Adam has affected us all, also remains a mystery, but it has. This state is evidenced by the compulsion to sin, John 8:34;

The focus on self. James 1:14-15.
The tendency to ignore what is right James 4:17.
Breaking God's laws. 1 John 3:4.
Doing that which you believe is not right. Romans 14:23.

Quite simply you never have to teach someone to do bad things, only good. It is also true that the redemption of the sinner is entirely a work of Jesus Christ. Unaided and un-accompanied he paid the price for the sin of the whole world.

> *And He Himself is the propitiation for our sins, and not for ours only but also for the whole world.* 1 John 2:2.

> *And you He made alive, who were dead in trespasses and sins, in which you once walked according to the course of this world, according to the prince of the power of the air, the spirit who now works in the sons of disobedience, among whom also we all once conducted ourselves in the lusts of our flesh, fulfilling the desires of the flesh and of the mind, and were by nature children of wrath, just as the others. But God, who is rich in mercy, because of His great love with which He loved us, even when we were dead in trespasses made us alive together with Christ, by Grace you have been saved, through faith, and that not of yourselves, it is the gift of God.* Ephesians 2: 1- 8.

Let me state it plainly. All have sinned both individually and as a result of being descendants from Adam. All are separated from God unless they have, by faith accepted the atonement of Jesus on their behalf. Salvation is entirely in every respect the work of Jesus Christ. No man can even believe, unless somehow, they are aided by the Holy Spirit.

Does this necessarily mean we are Utterly Depraved and there is no ability to respond to God, or to choose right or good in us? If we were to say, 'I have decided to follow Jesus,' does that amount to us aiding the work of redemption? If I exercise my will does that make me a contributor to my salvation?

How is the unbeliever dead? Ephesians 2:1-3

This is quite crucial here. What does 'dead' mean? Let us go back to Genesis 3:3. Adam was told he would die if he ate of the fruit of the tree of the knowledge of good and evil. But he did not physically die. The outcome was he was banished from the garden.3:24. Clearly death meant separation from God.

As we read on in Ephesians 2, we find the predicament of the gentile unbeliever was that they were aliens, strangers and foreigners to the household of God. Once again death means separation or exclusion, not total inability. In Ephesians 5:14 Paul equates the 'dead' with those who are sleeping. Stepping into a place of Grace is as one awakening from sleep, the senses that were at rest are galvanised once again to life.

In the parable of the Prodigal Son the story ends with this doublet.

Your brother was dead and is alive again, was lost and is found. Luke 15:32.

The word 'dead' is contrasted to the word 'alive,' and the word 'lost' is contrasted to the word 'found.' But at the same time the word 'dead' is equated with the word 'lost,' and the word 'alive' is equated with the word 'found.' 'Dead' did not mean 'totally unable,' but that he was lost to the father. In fact, he had some measure of ability, because he said, *'I will arise and go to my father and say to him, I have sinned.'* The wages of sin, is not death as in 'ceasing to exist,' but death as in 'eternal separation' from God. Romans 6:23.

What would be the case if someone should offer me a gift, unsolicited, undeserving and not as a reward or payment in kind, and I chose to accept that gift? What contribution to the nature of the gift does my acceptance make? Surely nothing at all. For even if I refused the gift, the gift remains essentially the same. It is not diminished if I refuse it, or embellished if I accept it. I therefore propose that an act of the will is not a contribution to the nature of salvation and that the exercise of the will is not meritorious in any way.

It may be true to say that 'I have decided to follow Jesus,' can be said with pride or a sense of achievement. But so can the belief that I have been randomly chosen by God for salvation. In fact, I would venture to say that the latter is more likely than the former. I can say, 'I have decided,' in humility, penitence, and gratitude.

The Composition of mankind.

We need to ask the question, is mankind composed of body and soul, or body soul and spirit. It is no surprise that the situation was complicated by the same characters we have quoted all along, Augustine and Pelagius. We do need to add another name, Apollinaris 310-390.

The early church fathers were predominantly believers in the three divisions of the human person, body soul and spirit. Apollinaris taught that Jesus had a human body and soul but not a human spirit. His spirit was the divine part of his nature. Pelagius's contribution was that the spirit of man was uncontaminated by sin and therefore able to respond to God. As we have seen, Augustine was always much exercised by Pelagius. His response on this matter was to say that the soul and the spirit of mankind were the same thing, so there could be no 'divine spark' within man waiting to be fanned into flame.

The reformers, following Augustine and others were all 'dichotomists' that is they believed in a body and soul only. They said that the terms spirit and soul are identical. It is therefore quite logical that from a historical perspective we have the word 'dead' meaning 'totally unable,' the soul is dead towards God, and mankind has no other spiritual capacity.

But we must ask again, are Augustine and his followers correct? Certainly, there are scriptures that suggest they are. Luke 1: 46-47. Sometimes mankind is described as body and soul, as in Matthew 10:28. In other places it is body and spirit. 1 Corinthians 5:3. The spiritual part of man that survives physical death is sometimes called spirit, 1 Peter 3:19 and at other times called soul, Revelation 6:9. One can be troubled in 'soul' John 12: 27; and troubled in 'spirit' John 13: 21. However, there are passages that describe man as body soul and spirit. 1 Thessalonians 5:23; Hebrews 4: 12.

We mentioned before the importance of the Church Fathers. What they heard was what the eyewitnesses said in the context in which it was said. What did they hear? Most commentators agree that the Church Fathers spoke of a body-soul-spirit composition of man. The following are examples.

Irenaeus 130-202;

> For that flesh which has been moulded is not a perfect man in itself, but the body of a man, and part of a man. Neither is the soul itself, considered apart by itself, the man; but it is the soul of a man, and part of a man. Neither is the spirit a man, for it is called the spirit, and not a man; but the commingling and union of all these constitutes the perfect man.

Irenaeus quoting Polycarp 69-155

> Man is a material body, his soul, in the classical sense, is his principle of life, and his spirit is that which orients him to be able to receive divinity. Man does not have God by nature, but he does image Him on each of the three aforementioned levels. He has the likeness of God by the Holy Spirit before the Fall and redemption is the process by which likeness is

restored and God's image in man is repaired. Christ is able to be perfect in image because He is fully man, having body, soul, and spirit and is perfect in likeness by His perfect receptivity of the Father's love as the Word.

In regard to the Holy Trinity. Sometimes the coupling of Father and Son are used. At other times, the Son and the Spirit, again the Father and the Spirit. On other occasions we have just one name of the trinity mentioned. Are we therefore to understand that because only one or two names of the trinity are mentioned that the trinity does not exist, or that they are referring to the same thing? I trust not. Whether it is the Father who speaks, or the Son, or the Spirit, we readily understand it is God who has spoken. In all cases, whichever name is in the actual text we know that all three eternally exist. I am not saying that man is a trinity like God is. God is a trinity of persons. Mankind maybe understood as a triunity. Therefore, to mention one or two parts of man's constitution does not exclude the existence of another. Furthermore, if the soul and spirit are recorded as doing the same, or similar, things it does not mean they are one. In the same way when the Holy Spirit says what the Son says, it does not mean they are one and the same person, just that they are engaged in the same matter.

The soul.

The soul is the life force in the physical body. It is what makes humans, although physically identical, totally unique from one another. A surgeon only has to study one human anatomy and he can operate on all. A psychiatrist needs to be aware of countless potential distortions of the mind, and even then, every patient is unique. *'Man became a living soul.'* It therefore can be said in this instance that man was a soul and had a body. We can sum up the nature of the soul by saying it is the seat of intellect, affections, and will. There are other words used, such as, heart, mind, flesh, nature, strength, and desires but they are all included in the same overall meanings. Sometimes the Bible refers to the soul as the person in their entirety. 1 Peter 3:20. The soul of the unbeliever can operate without reference to God. Luke 12:19. The soul can be aware of the need for God but cannot of itself do anything about it. Psalm 42:1-3. The soul on its own does not appreciate the things of God. 1 Corinthians 2:14-16.

The spirit.

We cannot deny there is similarity between the soul and spirit because they are at times engaged in the same practices. Luke 1: 46-47. We can say that the spirit also is composed of intellect, affections and will but not in regard to life on earth, despite modern parlance, but in relation to God.

The unbeliever is a living soul with a body and a somnolent or inactive spirit that needs awakening. The believer is a living soul with a body that has an awakened spirit that is now sensitive to the presence of God. The awakening of the spirit 'saves the soul' from its carnal self-centred desires and focuses it on the will and purposes of God, so the whole person is transformed.

It is difficult to determine if the spirit can be affected by sin. What is clear however, is that if the person is redeemed, then the whole person, spirit, soul and body are redeemed; and if a person is an unbeliever, then the whole person, spirit soul and body are lost. 2 Corinthians 7:1.

The spirit of man is the only thing that can honestly assess the value of the thoughts and intentions of the human heart. It is therefore essential in our communication with God. 1 Corinthians 2:11. The spirit of man is essential in the true confession of sin. Proverbs 20:27. The spirit of man links him to the Spirit of God so that he knows, senses and chooses things that are not as a result of a process of human learning.

Job 32:8-9.

> *That which is born of the flesh is flesh, and that which is born of the Spirit is spirit.* John 3: 6.

> *'God is Spirit, and those who worship Him must worship him in spirit and truth.'* John 4:24.

> *Do you not know that your bodies are members of Christ? Shall I then take the members of Christ and make them members of a harlot? Certainly not! Or do you not know that he who is joined to a harlot is one body with her? For the two, He says, shall become one flesh. But he who is joined to the Lord is one spirit with Him.* 1 Corinthians 6:15-17.

The acknowledgement of the spirit within mankind gives us the clue how man can respond to God without becoming part of salvation itself. The spirit of man is made for this purpose. Our spirit is awakened by this gift of faith which enables us to believe and step into the gift of Grace and be saved.

> *Therefore, it is of faith that it might be according to Grace. Romans 4:16.*

> *Therefore having been justified by faith we have peace with God through our Lord Jesus Christ.* Romans 5:1.

The spirit of man is particularly exercised in the operation of spiritual gifts. The *'spirit (of man) speaks mysteries.'* 1 Corinthians 14: 2. The spirit communicates with God on a level beyond human understanding. Things of God are revealed by the Holy Spirit. These can be kept in the individual's heart for their own edification or shared with a congregation. As a sign that the message is a word from God they are sometimes spoken in an unknown language and need another intervention of the Holy Spirit to interpret them into the common language. 1 Corinthians 14:1-5; 14-16. At other times this 'spirt (of man) to Spirit (The Holy Spirit)' communication is revealed directly in the common language.

He has set Eternity in our Hearts. Ecclesiastes 3:11.

> *The interpretation of 'eternity,' is conceived in the sense of a long indefinite period of time, in accordance with the use of the word throughout this book, and the rest of the Old Testament. God has placed in the constitution of man the capability of conceiving of eternity, the struggle to apprehend the everlasting, the longing after an eternal life.* [77]

The writer has just given us a description of the uncertainty, transience and instability of life, fluctuating from one experience to another. He then speaks of how this can cause the experiences of exasperation, despair, and melancholy. Yet in the midst of all this God has placed an awareness in the human heart for eternity. This awareness does not reveal God, and certainly does not save, but creates the restlessness to seek after God. By 'eternity' the writer implies something stable, lasting, superior and sublime. God has placed in mankind, despite his universal depravity, a longing for himself. Such longing can be explored or subdued, but it sits in the human spirit as a hope of the manifestation of the Grace of God. Romans 1:17.

> *The Spirit also bears witness with our spirit that we are children of God.* Romans 8:16

The Image of God.

The whole purpose of the Grace of God is to restore in mankind the Glorious Image of God. Mankind is not totally devoid of the Image of God in which he was created. Jesus said of Nathaniel that he was a man in whom there is no guile. John 1:47. Jesus asked the Ruler in Mark 10: 17-22, if he had

---

[77] Albert Barnes Commentary

kept the commandments? He said that he had, all of them, all his life. Jesus did not dismiss that as useless virtue, but it stirred in the Lord a compassionate reaction, '*He loved him.*' Mark 10:17-22. Although it appears that this man did not follow Jesus, at that time anyway, there was something in him that drew him to the Saviour, and something in the Saviour that drew him to the man.

The presence of the image of God is the reason why we believe in the sanctity of human life and exercise mutual respect. Everyone, believer or unbeliever bears the image of the creator and has the right to life. All mankind still possesses something of the 'image of God.' As this is the case, it seems to me, we cannot be totally or utterly depraved.

> *Whoever sheds man's blood, by man his blood shall be shed; for in the image of God, He made man.* Genesis 9: 6.

> *When I consider Your heavens, the work of Your fingers, the moon and the stars, which You have ordained, what is man that You are mindful of him, and the son of man that You visit him? For You have made him a little lower than the angels, And You have crowned him with glory and honour.* Psalm 8:3-4

Grace does not 'patch up' the distorted image that remains, but transforms us afresh to the standard of the original design. We are a 'New Creation' in Christ Jesus.
2 Corinthians 5:17

> *Just as we have borne the image of the man of dust, we shall also bear the image of the man of heaven.*
> 1 Corinthians 15:49.

> *And we all, with unveiled face, beholding the glory of the Lord, are being transformed into the same image from one degree of glory to another. For this comes from the Lord who is the Spirit.* 2 Corinthians 3:18.

You have put off the old self with its practices and have put on the new self, which is being renewed in knowledge after the image of its creator. Colossians 3:9-10.

The Grace Space

CHAPTER NINE

A fresh look at the Acts of Foreknowledge

In this chapter we are going to take a fresh look at the meaning and application of words such as, **Predestination, Election, Foreknowledge, Chosen.** I have called them the 'Acts of Foreknowledge' because they all describe acts of God before creation and consequently before the operation of human will. Scripture uses these words to describe the essential nature and source of the Plan of World Redemption. The outworking of these things in time is what we describe as salvation, transformation, being born anew and justification.

I wish to state that these words, as listed above, do not belong to Augustine, Calvin or the Reformed position on Grace. They belong to the New Testament. As such they are part of the '*corpus fidei*'[78] that is the experience of us all.

We return to the scriptures in Ephesians 1: 4-10 and pick out these pertinent words.

Chosen or Elect.

There is little substantial difference between the two words. *Chosen* can mean chosen out of a group as in purchasing an item, and *elect* can mean chosen to enter a group as in voting. But of course, you can choose to elect, and elect to choose. As such the words indicate to us that those who are saved are chosen from one group and elected into another. As there is no intermediate ground between the two, they describe one continuous act.

I think the important thing to note here is that we are **chosen in him.** 'In him' or a similar phrase occurs several times in this passage, depending on the translation. We are not chosen individually at random. We are chosen because of our relationship with Jesus Christ.

Verse 1 states that the book is written to the 'saints **in** Ephesus.' That is the corporate body of believers physically in that location. The common factor is that they are all in the same place. Then it says, '**in** Christ.' The common factor is the relationship they have to Jesus Christ. Everything said from now on is in regard to a corporate body of people in relationship with Jesus Christ. All of them, not individuals.

It is reflective of the Election of Israel. Israel was chosen as a nation because of the favour Abraham found with God. Genesis 15:18.; 1 Chronicles 16:14-19; Deuteronomy 7:7-8. Of course, individuals were chosen for specific tasks, but the nation was chosen because of Abraham. It could be said,

---

[78] Body of faith

'They were chosen in Abraham.' '*All Israel is not of Israel.*' Romans 9:6. This does not mean that some of Israel were not chosen in Abraham. It means that when the people of Israel faced the claims of Jesus Christ, some believed and some did not. Those that did not forfeited their place in the purposes of God.

Jesus is the Elect of God.

He was chosen individually to be the saviour. Isaiah 42:1; Matthew 12: 17-21; John 1:33-34. 1 Peter 2:6. We are only 'elect' because of our relationship with him.[79]

All the acts of foreknowledge; predestination, election, justification, glorification, were focused upon the process of bringing redemption to the world through Jesus Christ. This was pre-determined by God before the foundation of the world. As the programme unfolded in time, God called specific people to be involved in the process. Such as; Abraham Genesis 17:3-6; Israel, Deuteronomy 7:6-8; John the Baptiser, Luke 3: 16-17; as they became involved the acts of foreknowledge came to rest on them as well and, they were also known as the chosen or the elect, but only because of their incorporation into the plan.

Likewise, after the events of Calvary, the call to benefit from the Atonement Jesus secured, was sent to the whole world. Once again, those who responded also began to share in the chosen or elect status. Believers became the 'elect' because of their relationship with Jesus. Romans 8:17.

Faith precedes Grace

According to those that quote Calvin, Grace is the irresistible force that operates before we can believe and that brings us

---

[79] Elect in the Son Robert Shank

to faith. Hence the sacraments provide a space of Grace that stirs faith.

According to the scriptures, Faith is the persuasive force that brings us to Grace. Romans 4:16; 19-25. Abraham obtained his place of favour with God because he first believed the promise he had been given. Romans 5:1-4. We gain access to the Place of Grace by means of faith. The spirit of man is quickened as he believes what he has heard about Jesus. The first manifestation of Grace is the assurance of the forgiveness of sins and acceptance into the family of God.

In Luke 17: 19 *et al; Jesus* told the cleansed leper to '*go your way, your faith has made you well.*' This man, and the others Jesus healed, entered the place of Grace by means of his faith. In Matthew 8:10; 15:28, Jesus said that he had found great faith in the people concerned and as a result he brought them into a place of Grace. This process of enabling faith is the work of the Holy Spirit. We see in Stephen's sermon that the cause for unbelief was resistance to the Holy Spirit who was trying to induce faith in their hearts on the evidence of the risen Lord. Acts 7:51.

Grace and Faith are resistible. Mankind is neither compelled to, or deterred from believing.

> *O Jerusalem, Jerusalem, the one who kills the prophets and stones those who are sent to her! How often I wanted to gather your children together, as a hen gathers her chicks under her wings, but you were not willing!* Matthew 23:37.

Grace is the space where sins are forgiven, healing is received, Satan is overcome, blessings are received, and the purposes of God are fulfilled, and it is entered into by the gift of faith that God has made available to all. The Grace Space is really a foretaste of the age to come.

Foreknowledge.

Nothing in all creation is hidden from God's sight. Everything is uncovered and laid bare before the eyes of him to whom we must give account. Hebrews 4:13 N.I.V.

God knows everything, because he is eternal and all history lies before him at once in one great panorama. The disagreement comes from what God has done with that foreknowledge. Out of his foreknowledge he saw that creation would be contaminated by sin and Satan. He saw those in whom the gift of faith would operate in order to bring them into the place of Grace when it revealed the person of Jesus Christ.

It is important to note it is not the decision of individuals upon which future action would be based, but on the achievement of the gift of faith in the individual. Romans 8:28 presents foreknowledge as the basis of all that follows. To those he said, they will be my people.

He chose them on their response to the gift of saving faith.

He then prepared a destiny for them. A place wherein God and man could enjoy everlasting communion, free of sin, sickness and Satan.

He prepared a sacrifice for sin that could be potent enough to potentially eradicate the sin of all mankind.

He foresaw that everyone would not believe. That is, once again, not based on their decision so much as on the fact that the gift of faith would be ignored and hence rejected.

He prepared a place of eternal judgement for those who of their own free will had rejected faith and God's offer of grace.

He issued no decrees as to whom among mankind would be able to be saved and whom would not. For the sake of those who would believe, he offered Grace to all. Grace flows to the world not because God has decreed it but because he loved the world.

God foreknew those in every nation those who would believe, from the beginning of the world to the consummation of all things. but, in order to throw light upon this dark question, it should be well observed, that when we speak of God's foreknowledge, we do not speak according to the nature of things, but after the manner of men. For, if we speak properly, there is no such thing as either foreknowledge or after-knowledge in God. All time, or rather all eternity, (for the children of men,) being present to him at once, he does not know one thing in one point of view from everlasting to everlasting. As all time, with everything that exists therein, is present with him at once, so he sees at once, whatever was is, or will be, to the end of time. But observe: We must not think they are because he knows them. No: he knows them because they are. Just as I know the sun shines: Yet the sun does not shine because I know it, but I know it because it shines. My knowledge supposes the sun to shine; but does not in anywise cause it. In like manner, God knows that man sins; for he knows all things: Yet we do not sin because he knows it, but he knows it because we sin; and his knowledge supposes our sin, but does not in anywise cause it. In a word, God, looking on all ages, from the creation to the consummation, as a moment, and seeing at once whatever is in the hearts of all the children of men, knows every one that does or does not believe, in every age or nation. Yet what he knows, whether faith or unbelief, is in nowise caused by his knowledge. Men are as free in believing or not believing as if he did not know it at all.[80]

---

[80] *John Wesley, Sermon 58 – On Predestination*

Genesis 18: 16-33. The plea for Sodom.

We have here the remarkable account of Abraham's intercession for Sodom. '*Would you destroy the righteous with the wicked?*' Then the demonstration of God's Grace is exposed. Suppose 50, 45, 40, 30, 20, 10, people could be found in the city, would you save the city for that number of people. God said he would. It implies God works on the principle that he would extend Grace to all, so that he could save some.

Predestination.

Predestination to Life is the everlasting purpose of God, whereby (before the foundations of the world were laid) he hath constantly decreed by his counsel secret to us, to deliver from curse and damnation those whom he hath chosen in Christ out of mankind, and to bring them by Christ to everlasting salvation, as vessels made to honour. Wherefore, they which be endued with so excellent a benefit of God be called according to God's purpose by his Spirit working in due season: they through Grace obey the calling: they be justified freely: they be made sons of God by adoption: they be made like the image of his only begotten Son Jesus Christ: they walk religiously in good works, and at length, by God's mercy, they attain to everlasting felicity.[81]

Etymologically it means, set apart, ordain or appoint to a use beforehand. Predestination is a logical necessity to Choosing. It only occurs 4 times in the English New Testament. Romans 8:29, Romans 8:30, Ephesians 1:5 and Ephesians 1:11. The Greek word is used twice more, but translated as 'determined' in Acts 4:28, and 'ordained' in I Corinthians 2:7.

---

[81] Church of England 39 Articles

Romans 8: 29. '*Predestined to be conformed to the image of his son.*' What was determined beforehand was that those who had accepted Christ would bear the image of the character of Christ. They would be like him. 1 John 3:2.

Romans 8:30. Here we learn that those predestined would be called, justified, and glorified. They would be guaranteed a process of Grace that would change them to be like Jesus.

Ephesians 1:5. This tells us that the process of predestination would make us part of the family of God. '*Adopted as sons.*'

Ephesians 1:11-12. Predestination guarantees we will be '*for the praise of his glory.*' The process of redemption will ensure that those who have been saved will bring glory to God, because of what God has done in them.

> *In Him you also trusted, after you heard the word of truth, the gospel of your salvation; in whom also, having believed, you were sealed with the Holy Spirit of promise, who is the guarantee of our inheritance until the redemption of the purchased possession, to the praise of His glory.* Ephesians 1:13-14.

I fail to see from these verses that the word predestination has any application beyond the assurance that the process of Grace will transform people from unrighteousness to righteousness, guaranteed by the outpouring of the Holy Spirit which grants us glimpses of the glory of the age to come.

Hebrews 6:13-20. Based on the impossibility that God could lie, he has declared that

> *Those who have fled for refuge will lay hold of the hope set before them.*

I cannot see that it has anything to do with identifying a limited number of people and arbitrarily selecting them for salvation, while at the same time rendering everybody else incapable of believing. Charles Wesley wrote the following pertinent lines in regard to the predestation of the lost;

O Horrible Decree, worthy of whence it came!
Forgive their hellish blasphemy,
Who charge it on the Lamb.'
'To limit Thee they dare, blaspheme Thee to Thy face,
Deny their fellow-worms a share, in Thy redeeming grace.

In Paul's discussion on the salvation of the people of Israel in Romans 11, there is a phrase tucked away in verse 25.

`Until the fulness of the Gentiles has come in.'`

Most translations render it, *'The full number of the Gentiles.'* But this is not to say there are a specific number that must come in. Some years ago, my wife and I took a ferry ride on Ullswater in the Lake District of England. We were a little late and the boat had already sounded its horn to indicate it was ready to sail. We waved at the man in charge indicating we coming as quickly as possible. When we got to the boat, I apologised for keeping him waiting. He said to us they would never sail while they could see someone was on their way. And there is the truth. The Lord knows who will come and the door will not close until the last has made it home.

Does God ordain people to destruction?

Most people of the Reformed understanding today would deny this. I fear this denial is 'opportunistic' because it has been found, to promote the Reformed position as it was originally composed, is ethically indefensible. Maybe it is a longing that Calvin had actually reached different conclusions.

Much is made of the choice of God between Jacob and Esau.

> *Not only this, but when Rebecca also had conceived by one man, even by our father Isaac, (for the children not yet being born, nor having done any good or evil, that the purpose of God according to election might stand, not of works but of Him who calls), it was said to her, the older shall serve the younger. As it is written, Jacob I have loved, but Esau I have hated.* Romans 9:10-13.

This is very clearly God selecting a person for a specific role and rejecting another, not because of any qualities they displayed, because it was done before they were born. This is not a selection for salvation. Both were descendants of Abraham and recipients of the status as children of God and beneficiaries of the covenants with Israel. What had been at stake was the 'right of the firstborn' to be in the lineage of the Messiah. This Jacob had coveted and Esau despised. God foreknew this was to be the case, and his love and hate was expressed on this issue alone. Esau and his descendants became strangers to the Promises of God. They became the people of Edom and opponents of the descendants of Jacob. In fact, many Muslim people today see themselves as descendants of Esau and as a result believe that they are the authentic people of God, cheated out of their rightful status. Matters concerning the Messiah were pre-ordained. It had to be that way; the Messiah wasn't a position open for application. To apply the principles relating to the Messiah and apply them to everyone is a mistake that distorts the Grace of God.

> *What shall we say then? Is there unrighteousness with God? Certainly not! For He says to Moses, 'I will have mercy on whomever I will have mercy, and I will have compassion on whomever I will have compassion.' So, then it is not of him who wills, nor of him who runs, but of God who shows mercy. For the Scripture says to the Pharaoh, 'For this very purpose I have raised you up, that I may show My power in you, and that My*

name may be declared in all the earth.' Therefore, He has mercy on whom He wills, and whom He wills He hardens. You will say to me then, 'Why does He still find fault? For who has resisted His will? But indeed, O man, who are you to reply against God? Will the thing formed say to him who formed it, 'Why have you made me like this?' Does not the potter have power over the clay, from the same lump to make one vessel for honour and another for dishonour?

What if God, wanting to show His wrath and to make His power known, endured with much longsuffering the vessels of wrath prepared for destruction, and that He might make known the riches of His glory on the vessels of mercy, which He had prepared beforehand for glory, even us whom He called, not of the Jews only, but also of the Gentiles?
Romans 9:14-24

Truly God can do whatever he wants to do. But he has set himself certain parameters; justice, mercy, compassion, and truth and so on. God is infinitely ethical and moral. Therefore, there is no unrighteousness with God. God will dispense mercy and compassion **righteously not arbitrarily** on whoever he wills. There is no room here for arbitrary random privilege to some and not others.

Pharaoh is quoted as an example. When we read the story of the Exodus, we see there was a long process where Pharaoh resisted the call of God. Several times he asked Moses to intercede for him. Several times he promised to let the people go and then reneged on his decision. Exodus chapters 5-11. So, when it speaks of God hardening Pharaoh's heart, it was as a result of Pharaoh persistently hardening his own heart against the call of God. The 'hardening' is against the man who dares to argue with God. Pharaoh was likened to clay arguing with the potter. Isaiah 29:16; 45:9-10. This is someone who constantly rebels against God, someone who turns the creator/creature relationship upside down.

'*I have raised you up.*' God knew Pharaoh's heart. God knew he thought of himself as divine and ultimately would not acknowledge the God of Israel. Nevertheless, he granted him several opportunities to repent and become a partner with God in the great release of his people, as his forefather had been in the settling of the people there in the first place, but he would not.

Unlike Nebuchadnezzar much later, who also considered himself divine, he would not acknowledge that the God of Israel was God. Therefore, God allowed his arrogance to ripen to its fullest measure and hence righteously receive the judgments of God. '*He will have mercy on whom he will and whom he wills he hardens.*' God reserves the right to judge the persistently, unrepentant wicked.

'*Vessels of honour and vessels of dishonour.*' The potter alone decides what the clay will become without interference from the clay. This not saying that people are made for honour or dishonour. Where Paul is going here is in regard to the status of the people of Israel and gentile believers in the kingdom of God, as now established through Jesus Christ.

From the 'one lump of clay,' Israel, two distinct people have formed. Those who have believed Jesus, and those who have rejected Jesus. All had the opportunity to believe, but all did not. Those who had rejected Jesus had come from many generations of Jewish people who had rejected the call of God. But God was patient and longsuffering with them. They, like Pharaoh, all had the opportunities to believe. Hence it was within God's righteousness to reject descendants of Abraham from the Covenant of Calvary, because they rejected Jesus.

The display of the Righteous Judgements of God.

The Reformed position claims that the unrepentant sinner, 'non-elected' by God displays Gods righteous judgments as they are condemned to a Godless eternity. I think that the righteous judgments of God are displayed in the sufferings of

Jesus upon the Cross. No one can describe it better than the great prophet of Israel;

> *He is despised and rejected by men, a Man of sorrows*
> *and acquainted with grief. And we hid, as it were, our faces*
> *from Him; He was despised, and we did not esteem*
> *Him. Surely, He has borne our griefs and carried our sorrows;*
> *yet we esteemed Him stricken, smitten by God, and afflicted.*
> *But He was wounded for our transgressions, He was bruised*
> *for our iniquities; the chastisement for our peace was upon*
> *Him, and by His stripes we are healed. All we like sheep have*
> *gone astray; We have turned, every one, to his own way; and*
> *the Lord has laid on Him the iniquity of us all.* Isaiah 53:4-6.

The 'Decrees of God.'

> *The decrees of God are His eternal purpose according to the*
> *counsel of His will, whereby, for His own glory, He hath*
> *foreordained whatsoever comes to pass.*[82]

We have seen from Augustine and Calvin and their commentators, that the dominant descriptions of Grace have based everything on what they called the 'Decrees of God.' All made before the foundation of the world and outworked in due course in time. It insisted that the pivotal point in the distribution of Grace was in the decree not in the outworking. It is important to note that Paul said, *'He would glory in the Cross,'* the event on earth, in time, not in the decrees of God. It is stated that the decrees of God cannot take place after events because that would make God re-active, whereas he must always be pro-active. But surely, *'Where sin abounded, grace did much more abound,'* is a re-active statement.

In fact, the scriptures use the word 'decree,' as something that comes from God, establishing an irrefutable and irrevocable criterion, rarely, and then only in regard to the

---

[82] Baptist Catechism.

person and mission of Jesus, the order of creation and the restoration of Israel. In every other case the words decree, statue, law, ordinance, and such like refer to commandments which people are expected to keep, not laws whereby the human race is regulated.

We are told that the decrees regarding the Grace of God and salvation are, namely:-

The decree to create mankind.
The decree to permit the fall of mankind.
The decree to provide redemption.
The decree to choose certain people to accept redemption.
The decree to condemn everyone else to a lost eternity.

They can be arranged in three different orders which determine where in the sequence the 'lapse' or the 'fall' took place.'

> *By the decree of God, for the manifestation of his glory, some men and angels are predestined unto everlasting life, and others foreordained to everlasting death.*[83]

What has happened is, any declaration of God, covenant, ordinance, or promise, has been labelled a *decree*. These decrees have been made to cover all things in heaven, on earth and in hell. They are eternal and irrevocable, they concern every detail of everyone's life, they prescribe the choices a person will make, and determine the outcome of every situation that could possibly occur. Of particular interest to us is that they supposedly determine the parameters of Grace, whom it encompasses, and whom it passes by.

The pivotal point of salvation in this system, is located not in the events of Calvary, but in the pre-creation decrees. I repeat

---

[83] The Westminster Confession

that I do not see why it is necessary to list God's actions in sequence. The sequence of time is only important to us. Foreknowledge, choosing, predestining, calling, and justifying were all done in one instant of Redeeming Grace.

Berkhof, an eminent Reformed theologian of the highest order, nevertheless said;

> *There is, therefore, no series of decrees in God, but simply one comprehensive plan, embracing all that comes to pass. Our finite comprehension, however, constrains us to make distinctions, and this accounts for the fact that we often speak of the decrees of God in the plural. This manner of speaking is perfectly legitimate, provided we do not lose sight of the unity of the divine decree, and of the inseparable connection of the various decrees as we conceive of them. [84]*

There is an Eternal Purpose of God.

> *Therefore do not be ashamed of the testimony of our Lord, nor of me His prisoner, but share with me in the sufferings for the gospel according to the power of God, who has saved us and called us with a holy calling, not according to our works, but according to His own purpose and grace which was given to us in Christ Jesus before time began, but has now been revealed by the appearing of our Saviour Jesus Christ, who has abolished death and brought life and immortality to light through the gospel, to which I was appointed a preacher, an apostle, and a teacher of the Gentiles. For this reason, I also suffer these things; nevertheless, I am not ashamed, for I know whom I have believed and am persuaded that He is able to keep what I have committed to Him until that Day.* 2 Timothy 1: 8-12.

The Eternal purpose of God will culminate with the creation of a new heavens and earth.

---

[84] Louis Berkhof

But the day of the Lord will come as a thief in the night, in which the heavens will pass away with a great noise, and the elements will melt with fervent heat; both the earth and the works that are in it will be burned up. Therefore, since all these things will be dissolved, what manner of persons ought you to be in holy conduct and godliness, looking for and hastening the coming of the day of God, because of which the heavens will be dissolved, being on fire, and the elements will melt with fervent heat? Nevertheless we, according to His promise, look for new heavens and a new earth in which righteousness dwells.
2 Peter 3:10-13.

God will bring about his Eternal Purpose, not by a single deterministic thread of irrevocable law which he laid out before time, but by the amalgamation of several means, all under his ultimate sovereignty. His plan will be executed by the strength of his own arm, Luke 1: 49-55; the Covenant with the descendants of Abraham, Romans 11: 26-29; those redeemed by the Blood of the Lamb, Revelation 12: 10-12; and the kings of the earth. Psalm 2: 1-12.

- Sometimes God will accomplish what he wants done by exercising his authority and the desires of mankind are put aside. Isaiah 45: 9-10.
- Sometimes he will override the will of a person who has delegated authority, so that his will may be done. Numbers 24: 10-14.
- Sometimes he will persuade someone to use their delegated authority to do his will. Ezra 1:1
- Sometimes he will let mankind make free choices but he brings about his purposes through whatever option is chosen. 2 Samuel 24: 10-15.
- Sometimes he will launch an alternative history that replaces the will of man. Matthew 2:7-12.
- Believers are encouraged to earnestly seek the will of God before making decisions so that they choose in line with God's will. Romans `12:2.

- Whenever a person makes a choice that is contrary to the purposes of God, they will be held accountable for that decision and its consequences. Ezekiel 18: 1-18.

This does not sit easily with the philosophical reasoning of cause and effect, but it does more closely reflect the reality of the world in which we live.

Conclusions.

I would venture to say that the whole process of the acts of foreknowledge was motivated not by pure impassioned reason, but in the heart of a God who *loved* the world he had created and wished to restore it to its pristine condition. In the knowledge that some would respond, he offered Grace to all. What is certain is that no one who should be in his eternal kingdom will be barred from entering, and no one who should not be there will ever gain entrance!

Many commentators on Calvin and the 'Reformed Position' boast that the belief in unconditional particular election strengthens their evangelical message and fortifies the presentation of the gospel. I fail to see this.

The two outstanding evangelists of the 18th century, George Whitfield 1714-1770; and John Wesley 1703-1791, were Calvinist, and Arminian respectively. What they had in common, lacking in the scholarly reformers, was a passionate love for God and the same passionate love for the lost. It was this passion that got them out of the colleges, out of the churches, and on to the streets where the lost were, in order to announce to them the Good News about Jesus. It was this passion that the Holy Spirit was able to take and make their ministry effective.

Election of itself, is impassive. How can that endear one to God? It is no different than a number being chosen at random by a computer in a lottery. The result is very exciting but there is no affection shown to the computer or from the computer to the winner. The idea of being particularly chosen, mixed with human nature, is more likely to produce pride and an elitist attitude, not humility. The idea that I am loved and therefore chosen enforces the truth that my status is entirely down to the person of Jesus. God provided a Grace Space because he wanted to save as many of the sons and daughters of Adam who would care to believe.

The Grace Space

CHAPTER TEN

A fresh look at the Sacraments.

The sacraments have played a major role in the dispensing of Grace from New Testament times. We have seen how up to the Reformation, the sacraments were devised and administered to make the communicants totally dependent on the Church as a means of salvation. A right relationship with God and the hope of eternal life was only possible by participating in the sacraments relating to salvation, namely, baptism, confirmation, confession, penance, the eucharist, extreme unction and purgatory. This was largely the position from Augustine to the Reformation.

The reformers opposed this system. Grace was obtained through faith. Consequently, the sacramental system was dismantled by the reformers as they saw this as the heart of the problem. Although Luther was in favour of retaining a form of auricular confession, [85] it was not to be before a priest to gain Grace, or was it a sacrament. It was to rectify wrongs to seek reconciliation, and to obtain a clear conscience in the presence of a brother.

Luther, Calvin and Arminius each regarded that a sacrament had to have been instituted by Jesus Christ, contain a relevant outward display, and attain a real inner working of Grace. Based on the criterion above the reformers upheld Baptism and the Eucharist as legitimate sacraments. However, they were to be regarded as '*outward signs of an inner experience.*'

We would agree with Luther when he denied that Grace was imparted merely by the act of participation or the substance involved, it had to involve faith. Hence, immersion in water was an excellent demonstration of burial, (Romans 6:4). And bread and wine were excellent emblems of the body and blood of the Lord. Eating them was an excellent example of dependency of the believer on the sacrifice of Calvary. But Grace was imparted by faith, aided by the participation but only demonstrated in the substance. As the sacraments were taken directly from the Word of God, they carried that Word with them when they were performed, so they were instructions for future conduct. Consequently, a parent was obliged to raise their child in the faith after baptism, and people were expected to reflect a Christlikeness after the Eucharist. So, they deduced, as there was a real presence of Christ in the scriptures (John 5:39) so there was a real presence of Christ in the sacraments. Calvin put it like this;

A sacrament is an outward sign by which the Lord seals on our consciences the promises of his good will toward us in order to sustain the weakness of our faith; and we in turn attest our piety toward him in the presence of the Lord and of his angels and

---

[85] Private confession of sins to a priest

before men. [86]

Calvin also defined the sacrament as, '*a visible sign of a sacred thing.'*

Baptism.

Arminius taught that the baptism of the child of parents already in the Covenant of Grace was the normal and regular form of baptism. However, he did allude to baptism of older people if they were converted later in life.

Both Luther and Calvin promoted Paedo-Baptism.[87] They argued that baptism revealed the promise of salvation and should be conferred on the children of people already in a state of Grace. It was to be in the form of sprinkling water over the child. There was some latitude given to Credo-Baptism [88] for people who came to faith as adults. I am puzzled to know what persuaded men like Luther and Calvin to adopt Paedo-Baptism when they were otherwise so devoted to '*Sola Scriptura ?* '

The reformers position on Predestination meant that baptism washed away the sins of the elect child. There seemed to be a notion that the child born within the faith was more likely to be among the elect than one born outside the faith. The child that subsequently grew up in the faith was proof that they were elect and that they stood in a place of Grace from baptism. Calvin taught that baptism follows faith, but of course, the faith in question was decreed in eternity and the sacrament was just the outworking of that in time. This was their sacrament of Baptism which they vehemently defended. The presence of faith was as a result of God's decrees, not

---

[86] Institutes of the Christian Religion (IV.xiv.1-2)

[87] Infant baptism

[88] From credo, to know; baptism with knowledge of what one was doing.

personal choice. This is at variance to the apparent practice of the Church Fathers, as we have already noted.

> *But before the baptism, let the baptizer fast, and also the baptized, and whatever others can; but thou shall order the baptized to fast one or two days before.* [89]

> *As many are persuaded and believe that what we teach and say is true, and undertake to live accordingly, are instructed to entreat God with fasting...then they are brought by us where there is water, and are regenerated in the same manner in which we ourselves were...For Christ also said: 'Unless you be born-again, you cannot see the kingdom of God.* ' [90]

> *They who are about to enter baptism ought to pray with repeated prayer, fasts, and bendings of the knee, and vigils all the night through, and with the confession of all bygone sins, that they may express the meaning of the baptism of John.* [91]

Here baptism followed conversion and instruction and was a public confession and an outward sign of the inner state of Grace that had been already obtained by faith. The decision to believe and be baptised is clearly the decision of the individual concerned. This is clearly portrayed in Acts 8: 30-38. If this is what the first generation after the eyewitnesses heard, then we can be sure that this what they were told. Baptism after conversion and instruction was the original form of baptism.

What are we to make of this? The New Testament only gives details of Credo-baptism, and mere hints at Paedo-baptism. The Church Fathers practiced Credo-Baptism, yet by the 4th century the form and the significance of baptism had changed so that the baptism of infants was the norm. The strange thing

---

[89] Didache 100.
[90] Justin the Martyr
[91] Tertullian

is there is no record of a theological debate about it as there is about almost everything else.

To unravel this conundrum, we need to return once again to Augustine.

> *Now, inasmuch as infants are not held bound by any sins of their own actual life, it is the guilt of original sin which is healed in them by the grace of Him who saves them by the laver of regeneration.* [92]

Augustine stated that the faith of the child was absent due to their age, but that it was replaced by the faith of the parents. If the child turned out to be among the elect then the faith of the parents would have acted on behalf of the child until the child could express faith for itself. The idea that the faith of one person can save another is derived from the Catholic idea of the 'deferred grace' of the saints we have mentioned earlier. [93]

The important thing here is that Augustine attached a theological reason to the practice of baptising infants. Up until this point it is quite likely that infants had been baptised when the parents came to faith and were baptised. The uncertainty of the times indicated that this was expedient. As we have said, there was the notable difference in that the early Fathers were mostly dealing with new converts of all ages, whereas by the 4th century they were largely dealing with children born into the faith.

It would seem there was a gradual move to Paedo-Baptism in

---

[92] Augustine. A Treatise on the Merits and Forgiveness of Sins, and on the Baptism of Infants.

[93] Chapter 3; Purgatory; chapter 4; Sovereignty of God; chapter 5; The Reformers

the absence of theological debate. It would seem to me the change was more down to the circumstances of the times than a theological position. In addition to Augustine's explanation of the expiation of Original Sin there was added the belief that baptism was a rite of passage into the church, the family of God.

> *So that children believe, not by their own act, but by the faith of the Church, which is applied to them: by the power of which faith, grace and virtues are bestowed on them.* [94]

Baptism had now changed from a confession of faith, to the washing away of Original Sin and entrance to the church, as long of course, that the child was elect.

Did Paedo-Baptism deal with sin inherited from Adam?

In the 21st century, in the western world, we find this idea of original sin difficult to contemplate, it is mainly because today, we are so autonomous and individualistic. We have difficulty identifying with a nation because our nations are so multi-ethnic. We have difficulty identifying with a tribe, clan or family. Families are not homogenous any more. We are geographically and ideologically scattered. You can have different religions, different political views, different ethnicities, all in one family. As a result, many people have opted for individualism, and stand-alone from identifiable groupings.

Some years ago, while visiting Zambia, a group of church ministers asked me, what tribe did I belong to? I was stunned by their question. All I could think to reply was that I was British. I didn't have a tribe. They were as stunned by my answer as I was by their question. Although they were all

---

[94] Thomas Aquinas. *Summa Theologiae* Q 69, A 6.

devoted followers of Jesus Christ, they knew what tribe they came from and the corporate responsibilities that knowledge carried.

What I am getting at is that the Bible was written by people with a very strong consciousness of tribal or national identity. Above all was the corporate oneness of all humanity. It was therefore perfectly acceptable to say that the federal head of humanity has affected the outcome of humanity.

> *And He has made from one blood every nation of men to dwell on all the face of the earth, and has determined their pre-appointed times and the boundaries of their dwellings, so that they should seek the Lord, in the hope that they might grope for Him and find Him, though He is not far from each one of us; for in Him we live and move and have our being, as also some of your own poets have said, 'For we are also His offspring.'* Acts 17:26-28.

As a result, when God views humanity in regard to salvation he sees one vast tribe, all affected by sin in the same fundamental way,

> *All have sinned and come short of the glory of God.* Romans 3:23.

And we are right to protest that it had nothing to do with us. And God agrees. So, he devised a way of salvation which also had nothing to do with us. The first estate, we were born into by the choice of another, the second estate we can be born into by the actions of another.

I would contend that parents have no need to rush to get their child baptised in case they die before they come to an age of responsibility. It will do no harm if they do, and if it is done in the sincerity of faith, it will be a good and beneficial thing. Sadly, I fear, that is not the usual scenario. Whatever, Paedo-Baptism is not going to eradicate Adam's sin. Jesus cancelled the effect of Adam's sin on the Cross. The child is born covered by the Covenant of Calvary, whether the parents believe or not. Jesus is the second Adam.

> *For as in Adam all die, even so in Christ all shall be made alive.* 1 Corinthians 15: 22.

That means as Adam stood in relation to all mankind; he sinned we all sin, so Jesus stands in relationship to all mankind; as he was righteous, we too can be righteous through him.

The difference however is that our relationship to Adam is generational, our relationship to Jesus is by choice.

> *But the free gift is not like the offense. For if by the one man's offense many died, much more the grace of God and the gift by the grace of the one Man, Jesus Christ, abounded to many. And the gift is not like that which came through the one who sinned. For the judgment which came from one offense resulted in condemnation, but the free gift which came from many offenses resulted in justification.* Romans 5: 15-16.

We do not enter the place of Grace as one mass of humanity, we enter as individuals. There is sufficient space for all, and all may come, but we can only come because we are enabled, and take advantage of that enabling, and choose to believe.

That is the wonderful Grace of God. Christ has provided a Grace Space sufficient for everyone. John Stott calls it '*the sphere of Grace.*' [95] Regretfully, many of these Grace-Spaces are vacant because when people become of a maturity to understand what Jesus has done, they chose their own way and stepped out of the Grace Space.

Grace did not fail, the space remains. But the person began

---

[95] John Stott. The Message of Romans. TBST series.

to accumulate their own transgressions and drift away from God. These transgressions have now separated us from God and must be dealt with. God comes again in Grace and enables us by the Holy Spirit to believe. Then through confession and repentance we step into our Grace Space. Now it is time to be baptised as a public demonstration of what has happened in our hearts and to declare that it is our intention to follow Jesus all the days of our life, by means of his Grace.

The Grace of God provided at Calvary was sufficient to take away the power, guilt and shame of Adam's accumulative sin, and the transgression of our own volition. Grace is not meted out to us in bits and drabs as we perform pious acts. It is available in all its fulness the moment we accept Jesus. Fallen human nature fails constantly, but Grace is big enough for us to return to the Cross to rectify the matter. 1 John 1:9.

Spiritual Circumcision?

The idea that baptism signified our entrance into the church is based on the idea that it is an equivalent act to circumcision.

> *In Him you were also circumcised with the circumcision made without hands, by putting off the body of the sins of the flesh, by the circumcision of Christ, buried with Him in baptism, in which you also were raised with Him through faith in the working of God, who raised Him from the dead. And you, being dead in your trespasses and the uncircumcision of your flesh, He has made alive together with Him, having forgiven you all trespasses, having wiped out the handwriting of requirements that was against us, which was contrary to us. And He has taken it out of the way, having nailed it to the cross.*
> Colossians 2:11-14.

These verses, at first glance, seem to create a link between circumcision and baptism. Baptism being *'the circumcision without hands.'* I find it difficult to see that link because for one thing circumcision was something done only to males, whereas baptism is for all. Circumcision is a mark of ethnic solidarity and a mark of bearing the blessings and responsibilities of God's covenant with Abraham their father. It was a 'sign and seal' of Abraham's faith. Romans 4:11. But it didn't transform the lives of all who subsequently received it. Romans 9:6.

However, baptism is a sign and seal of a better covenant, one that transforms mankind from the heart. Circumcision leaves a mark on the flesh. Baptism leaves no mark on the flesh but a transformation of the heart. Circumcision shows identity with Abraham, baptism shows identity with Christ. Abraham was commended not because he was circumcised but because he possessed faith.

> *Does this blessedness then come upon the circumcised only, or upon the uncircumcised also? For we say that faith was accounted to Abraham for righteousness.*
> *How then was it accounted? While he was circumcised, or uncircumcised? Not while circumcised, but while uncircumcised. And he received the sign of circumcision, a seal of the righteousness of the faith which he had while still uncircumcised, that he might be the father of all those who believe, though they are uncircumcised, that righteousness might be imputed to them also, and the father of circumcision to those who not only are of the circumcision, but who also walk in the steps of the faith which our father Abraham had while still uncircumcised.* Romans 4: 9-12.

The equivalent of circumcision in the New Testament is not baptism, but sanctification. That is, the process of becoming Christlike.

> *For he is not a Jew who is one outwardly, nor is circumcision that which is outward in the flesh; but he is a Jew who is one inwardly; and circumcision is that of the heart, in the Spirit, not in the letter; whose praise is not from men but from God.* Romans 2: 28-29.

Was Baptism an act of regeneration?

This is the idea that the act of baptism was regenerative in itself, that is, it brought the child to salvation and into the family of God. There are those who believe that Credo-Baptism is also regenerative and that a person it not saved unless they are baptized.

To this I would respectfully say, there can be no act, sacramental or not, wherein the act itself is regenerative. If we allow this, we will go down the route of idolatry where specific procedure or ritual must be followed to appease God. The spiritual benefit must be an inner work of the Holy Spirit. Worship is to be in '*Spirit and Truth*' irrespective of location and beyond the minutiae of procedure. John 4:21-24.

The physical act of redemption was accomplished and finished by the work of Christ on the Cross of Calvary. Sacraments are only signs that point forwards, as does baptism, or backwards as does the Eucharist.

Anabaptists.

This means 'second baptism.' It was a name given to a group of reformers who said that Paedo Baptism was of no purpose or value. It was part of the superstitions that the Reformation was dismantling. Therefore, anyone who came to know Christ through faith in the Word of God, needed to be re-baptised after their conversion.

They were vehemently criticised by the more prominent Reformers and considered heretical. To be re-baptised became a crime in certain regions and it was not unknown for proponents of the belief to be executed. To be fair, certain Anabaptist groups did adopt unacceptable moral practices. They claimed the New Testament text and the practice of the Church Fathers as their authentication. They generally held a high view of scripture and its literal interpretation. They advocated living in separate communities. They became the fore-fathers, on the matter of baptism, of the Baptist churches, the various Brotherhoods, most Evangelical and Pentecostal Churches.

> *Baptism shall be given to all those who have learned repentance and amendment of life, and who believe truly that their sins are taken away by Christ, and to all those who walk in the resurrection of Jesus Christ, and wish to be buried with Him in death, so that they may be resurrected with Him and to all those who with this significance request it (baptism) of us and demand it for themselves. This excludes all infant baptism, the highest and chief abomination of the Pope. In this you have the foundation and testimony of the apostles.* Matt. 28, Mark 16, Acts 2, 8, 16, 19.[96]

Baptism was effected, either by full immersion or by pouring a significant amount of water over the candidate.

The grace of Baptism is manifest in the following way.

The Likeness of His death. Romans 6: 3

'*We were baptised into his death.*' The death of Jesus marked the end of an era. '*It is finished.*' The suffering was finished. The cup of sorrows was filled to the brim. When the stone was rolled over the door of Joseph's tomb, he would suffer no more. Neither need anyone else suffer for sin. His sum of sufferings was the equivalent to every man and woman being individually punished for their sin. His righteousness and innocence were equivalent to every man and woman standing in sinlessness before God. He had displayed for all to see that the righteous judgements of God are not to be trifled with. Yet his sufferings were not for his own sin but for ours. Isaiah

---

[96] Schleitheim Confession 1527

53: 4-6. There are few things that can motivate the human heart towards goodness. The one that achieves it the most is the knowledge that someone has laid down their life for someone else. If that does not motivate us to turn to God, then nothing will.

> *Why should he love me a sinner undone;*
> *Why, tell me why should he care?*
> *I do not merit the love he has shown.*
> *Why, tell me why should he care?*
> *All my iniquities on him were laid;*
> *He nailed them all to the tree.*
> *Jesus, the debt of my sin fully paid,*
> *He paid the ransom for me.* [97]

We take our first steps into the Place of Grace when we accept that Jesus died for me. This is the acknowledgement that salvation is entirely a work of the Grace of God and nothing of mankind.

> *For the love of Christ compels us, because we judge thus: that if One died for all, then all died; and He died for all, that those who live should live no longer for themselves, but for Him who died for them and rose again.* 2 Corinthians 5: 14-15.

The Grace of baptism is bestowed in that we are submerged into a realm where we cannot naturally survive. If we were to stay there our senses would cease to operate. We are under the water but for a moment, but it is enough to make the sign. As the effect of sin on the Lord Jesus ceased at Calvary, so the consequence of sin over our lives is pronounced to be broken in the sign of the Grace of Baptism. We 'entered death' but there was no judgment, pain, or sentence. Symbolically we went where Jesus went, but there was nothing to hold us there because the guilt of sin had been cancelled.

---

[97] J M Moore 1925-2017

The Likeness of His resurrection Romans 6:5.

We will skip over the burial for now. Let us look at the *'Likeness of His Resurrection.'* Jesus rose from the dead. Death could not hold him. Death had no power to hold him because he was without sin and death only had jurisdiction over the ones who have sinned.

When we are raised from the water, we pronounce the sign that we have come back to life because death cannot hold us either. But it is not the old life, as the life Jesus lived after the resurrection was dynamically different form the life he lived before, so our life is now also dynamically different. We enter another dimension of Grace. Our lives are opened to a spiritual dimension that was unknown to us beforehand. Jesus ascended to the Father and we can ascend to the Father through our relationship with Jesus, in prayer and worship. It is a guarantee that at the end of the age the dead in Christ will be restored and the living believer will be transformed in the likeness of His resurrection, to die no more.

The Likeness of His Burial. Romans 6: 4.

We were *'buried with Him.'* The burial of Christ covers a short period of time. The moment a person is submerged signifies this period of time. The scriptures are not clear on what was going on in this period. It seems that the best understanding is that Jesus was doing something regarding the faithful and unfaithful who lived before him. For our purposes here I simply want to emphasise separation. The life that was lived before was separated from the life lived after. We have not evolved into a better life through discipline, penance, or education.

> *Could it be any clearer that our former identity is now and forever deprived of its power? For we were co-crucified with him to dismantle the stronghold of sin within us, so that we would*

not continue to live one moment longer submitted to sin's power. Obviously, a dead person is incapable of sinning. And if we were co-crucified with the Anointed One, we know that we will also share in the fullness of his life.
Romans 6:6-8 Passion translation.

And thanks be to God, for in the past you were servants of sin, but now your obedience is heart deep, and your life is being moulded by truth through the teaching you are devoted to. And now you celebrate your freedom from your former master—sin. You've left its bondage, and now God's perfect righteousness holds power over you as his loving servants.
Romans 6: 17-18. Passion translation.

The Grace of God has exposed us to higher influences. We are inspired to Christlikeness and dis-engaged from unrighteousness. The deep motivation of our heart has been changed.

Christ's resurrection is your resurrection too. This is why we are to yearn for all that is above, for that's where Christ sits enthroned at the place of all power, honour, and authority! Yes, feast on all the treasures of the heavenly realm and fill your thoughts with heavenly realities, and not with the distractions of the natural realm.
Your crucifixion with Christ has severed the tie to this life, and now your true life is hidden away in God in Christ.
Colossians 3:1-3. Passion translation.

Yes, God raised Jesus to life! And since God's Spirit of Resurrection lives in you, he will also raise your dying body to life by the same Spirit that breathes life into you!
Romans 8:11. Passion translation.

This is the mystery of Grace. In the darkness of the tomb the broken body of our Saviour was transformed into the resurrection body of our Lord. As for us, the heart is changed. We are a new creation. We have experienced the real presence of Christ. We have a desire for the things of the Holy

Spirit. Baptism points forward to a life to be lived for the Glory of God.

The Eucharist.

The Eucharist, Communion, Lord's Supper, Mass, or Breaking of Bread emerged from a form of the Passover Jesus celebrated with the disciples before the crucifixion. It became part of church practice at the command of the Lord himself.

There were several prominent views of the Eucharist as the Reformation evolved. The traditional view that had evolved from Augustine was that the bread and wine were physically and permanently transformed into the actual body and blood of the Lord. Hence, they could never leave the altar and any leftovers had to be consumed by the priest or reserved for the housebound. The bread and wine still held the appearance of bread and wine but a mysterious transformation had taken place during the prayer of consecration.

It seems that the Reformers' views emerged from an over-reliance on interpreting John 6:41-59 as a commentary on the Eucharist. If anything, these verses are commentary on the meaning of the feeding of the 5000, and are using the miracle of the manna as an illustration of the work of Christ. As for the 'eating of his flesh and the drinking his blood' is that not best explained as an allegory based on 1 Chronicles 11:19? David's men were no more literally drinking his blood and eating his flesh than Jesus' audience was. David was remarking about how those men had risked their lives (their flesh and blood) for him. The message being, salvation is obtained by total dependence on Jesus and by taking advantage of the salvation he offers at his expense.

Luther believed that the bread and wine remained so, but were filled with the real presence of Christ, but only for the duration of the sacrament.

Ulrich Zwingli, (1484-1531) whom we have not quoted previously, held the view that the Eucharist was merely a memorial when we remembered what Christ had done but there was no transformation of any kind.

Calvin was not so clear on the subject and seemed to try and amalgamate all views into one. His definition of a sacrament, *'visible sign of a sacred thing, or a visible form of an invisible grace,'* was straightforward. But other comments were not.

> *So, sacraments in action alone to Calvin are nothing in themselves, just as seals of a diploma or a public deed are nothing in themselves, and would be affixed to no purpose if nothing was written on the parchment.* [98]

It seems that Calvin leaned in the direction of Zwingli but held to a mystical presence of the Lord, but not a change of the substance of the bread and wine. As a result, history has evolved in that the Reformed Churches and the Orthodox Churches tend to follow Luther and preserve a solemn ceremony. Evangelical and Pentecostal churches seem to favour Zwingli and the ceremony is less formal, sometimes quite casual. Those that practice a more solemn ceremony tend to capture the mystery of Christ's Presence. Those who treat it less formally tend to lose the sense of mystery and awe and the whole thing becomes very superficial.

How do we find Grace in the Eucharist?

> *For I received from the Lord that which I also delivered to you: that the Lord Jesus on the same night in which He was betrayed took bread; and when He had given thanks, He broke it and said, Take, eat; this is My body which is broken for you; do this in remembrance of Me. In the same manner He also took the cup after supper, saying, this cup is*

---

[98] Calvin The Institutes of the Christian Religion.

the new covenant in My blood. This do as often as you drink it, in remembrance of Me.

For as often as you eat this bread and drink this cup, you proclaim the Lord's death till He comes.

Therefore, whoever eats this bread or drinks this cup of the Lord in an unworthy manner will be guilty of the body and blood of the Lord. But let a man examine himself, and so let him eat of the bread and drink of the cup. For he who eats and drinks in an unworthy manner eats and drinks judgment to himself, not discerning the Lord's body. For this reason, many are weak and sick among you, and many sleep. For if we would judge ourselves, we would not be judged. But when we are judged, we are chastened by the Lord, that we may not be condemned with the world.

Therefore, my brethren, when you come together to eat, wait for one another. But if anyone is hungry, let him eat at home, lest you come together for judgment. And the rest I will set in order when I come. 1 Corinthians 11:23-34.

Certain words stand out. Remembrance; Proclaim; Examine; Unworthy; Judgment; Discernment; and Condemnation. Without examining the meaning of each word, we can determine the following;

The Eucharist is a Memorial of Christ's Death.

It is designed to continually bring before our minds the events of Calvary, ensuring that the focal point of all Christian worship is the Cross. But it is more than just a recalling of the event. It is in line with the Passover concept of '*We were there.*' In the part of the ceremony that follows the second cup, the cup of deliverance, Exodus 13:8, the '*Haggadah*' [99] service reads;

And you shall tell your son in that day, saying, "This is done because of what the Lord did for me when I came up from Egypt."

---

[99] The order of service for the Passover

The peculiar use of the first person in the Hebrew text, is taken to mean that the participant in the Passover must fulfil the ceremony *'as if he were there.'* We therefore must contemplate, he washes my feet, and he shares the bread and wine with me. At this moment, I am not seen as one of the Elect, or even a member or minister of a Church, but an individual for whom Christ died. It is a place of Grace where I can stand and observe another suffer for my sin. I see the lightning flash of Divine wrath and the thunder of righteous judgment, but it doesn't strike me, it strikes the Saviour. We take the bread and wine and there is a transformation that ensues. It is more of a transfiguration. Not of the bread and wine, but of ourselves. We become one with the Lord as he walks the Calvary Road. Without pain, distress, or the weight of sin, our Lord bears all that, but we walk through it with him nevertheless.

The Eucharist is a Proclamation of a current Condition.

For as often as you eat this bread and drink this cup, you proclaim the Lord's death till He comes.

The Grace is found in the proclamation of the Lord's death. The proclamation is *'He died for me.'* The emphasis shifts slightly from the Lord's death, to what the Lord's death has accomplished in those who have participated. The verse closes with the clause, *'until he comes.'* This proclamation will echo on, from generation to generation and the testimony will be the same. The declaration is that the death of Christ remains as efficacious as it was at the beginning for whoever will call upon the Name of the Lord. In the words of the hymnwriter, C H Morris, *'and the blood has never lost its power, no never!*

The Eucharist is an act of Solemn Self Examination.

Here I would tend to diverge from Zwingli in favour of Luther. These words are so severe, so solemn, that to treat this ceremony casually or flippantly is a mistake. Both spiritual and physical life and death are at stake.

An Anglican Priest with whom I was once acquainted said to me, *'The power of God is in the mystery of the Eucharist.'* I have come to believe he was right. When everything is laid out and explained, well, that's it, it is explained, and we can understand. But so often by understanding we distil the mystery and reduce the power. There are mysteries in Grace that are best left as mysteries if we are going to benefit from them. Quite how one partakes unworthily, I am not sure. Quite how such action leads to sickness and death I am not sure. But the words are clearly cautionary. So, I leave that for what it is and make sure that I approach the Eucharist in awe, sobriety, and with gravitas, because it is precarious ground.

To make sure we are standing in Grace at the moment we are called upon to examine ourselves. It is the 'true confessional.' We are to ask God what there is in us that sent him to the cross, confess it, repent of it, and vow to leave it behind, and so we take the bread and wine. Whatever the warnings mean this is the way we can be sure we are standing in the place of Grace.

This is also the 'true penance.' We are *'Chastened of the Lord.'* It is not the performing of some arduous or painful task prescribed by a priest. It is the chastening of the Lord. It can be the conviction of the spirit of man. It can be when we are troubled within because something is wrong. It can be the consequences of our actions. Not the guilt, that has been atoned for, but things that we have done or said can still roll on in circumstances and the lives of people long after we have repented of it.

Finally, we '*wait for one another.*'

The Eucharist is ideally a communal activity. In the Eucharist we are to bear in mind that each person is, or should be, going through what has been described. Don't rush it. Give time for the Lord to deal with each one individually. Obviously, the clause is related to the somewhat raucous practice of the Corinthians hinted at in earlier verses. However, it remains for us to bear with those who have much to sort out with God. I must ensure that I not only stand in the place of Grace, but those around me stand there as well.

These are the things that matter. What doesn't matter is whether wine or grape juice is used; whether leavened or unleavened bread is used; whether you do it daily, weekly or monthly; or whether it is led by a priest, pastor or a fellow brother or sister in Christ.

I would contend that the Eucharist is a sacrament, and that in the way described, the real presence of Christ can be experienced. The transformation is in the heart of the believer not in the bread and wine.

The Grace Space

CHAPTER ELEVEN

Discovering the dimensions of Grace

Then you will be empowered to discover what every holy one experiences—the great magnitude of the astonishing love of Christ in all its dimensions. How deeply intimate and far-reaching is his love! How enduring and inclusive it is! Endless love beyond measurement that transcends our understanding—this extravagant love pours into you until you are filled to overflowing with the fullness of God!
Ephesians 3:18-19 The Passion Translation.

In this chapter we will consider a selection of Bible characters who in remarkable ways discovered the measureless Grace of God; its height, depth, and width. I have selected these stories in particular, not because they are somehow superior to others accounts, but because they have impacted me personally. I intend to show how the experiences of these Bible characters have added to the revelation of the Immaculate Grace of God.

Noah. *Genesis 6-9.*

Grace shining in a dark place

Noah found Grace in the eyes of the Lord. Genesis 6:8. The eyes of the Lord were focused on the wickedness of man. God saw that mankind was wholly intent on wickedness. He saw that there had been cohabitation with what appears to be demonic beings that threatened to genetically corrupt the human race. Respect for life and property had evaporated. Genesis 6:13. God was grieved, that is, he was in great pain and turmoil and He determined to eradicate the creation he had made. It seems also that mankind had begun to see themselves as gods. In Genesis 4: 26, it seems to say that men began to call upon the name of the Lord in worship. Many commentators interpret it in this way. If this is so it would indicate a propagation of true religion. However, the tone of the next two chapters is morally and spiritually downward, not upward. Rabbinical commentators see this as the dawn of apostasy.[100] The text could be better read as, '*They called themselves by the name of the Lord.'* Which would imply they saw themselves as gods.

A man or woman observing the rising waters and the devastation it was causing would perceive the face of an angry God. But Noah looked at the face of God and saw something else; Grace. Noah found Grace in his perception of God. If we can for a moment literalise the concept of the 'face of God' we would see, like Noah, behind the fierce righteous anger, a heart of Grace.

The flood judgment was irrevocable and inevitable. Nothing was going to delay or avert it. Noah proclaimed the coming judgment and the means of surviving it for 120 years. Genesis

---

[100] David Parsons Floodgates.

6:3; Hebrews 11:7; 2 Peter 2:5. It is implied that Noah invited people to join him in His project but no one listened and no one cared. This apathy is startling when we consider that according to the ages of the men mentioned, Adam would have still been alive in the lifetime of Lamech, Noah's father. Taking Genesis 6:3 to mean that the flood would come after 120 years Noah would have begun to build the ark 20 years before his sons were born. None of the men listed in Genesis 5, including his own father, involved themselves in the project. No one else, except, presumably, his own immediate family, saw Grace in the face of God. Noah was unique in his generation. Genesis 6:9. '*he walked with God.*'

Adam had walked with God but surrendered his privilege. Enoch walked with God and was translated from earth to heaven. Enoch was taken away because his faith and righteousness had angered those around him. Jude 14-15. His life was in danger so God took him away so that he would avoid death. I don't actually think it meant Enoch did not die, but rather his death was in God's hands, not the hands of his enemies. Be that as it may. Everyone, including Adam would have observed it, but it meant nothing to them. So deep was the depravity. In the unimaginable darkness of that time Noah walked with God and found a place of Grace.

Alongside this, God instructed Noah to build a 'Grace Space.' It was a boat wherein those that believed in God and had not been contaminated with the wickedness of the age would be preserved. While the depraved wickedness of mankind and the righteous judgment of God collided in violent judgment around him, Noah, his family, and a large company of animals were safe in the Grace Space. The Grace Space is that place where we are sheltered from the righteous anger of God and the depraved wickedness of mankind.

This illustration is particularly pertinent to us because Jesus said that the days of the coming of the Son of Man would be comparable to the days of Noah. Matthew 24:36-44. These days will be marked by hedonism, debauchery, demonic activity, and ignorance of the things of God. Mankind in general will have no knowledge of, or interest in, the urgency of the hour. They will be oblivious as to whom God considers righteous and whom he considers wicked. So much so that two people working side by side will appear identical until the Day of the Lord breaks. Then one will be taken away to judgment and the other will enter the Kingdom to come. It will be a total and utter surprise to the wicked. The one is in the Grace Space and the other is not. Two women at the mill and two men in the field will look towards the heavens, one man and one woman will see nothing at all, the others' will have found Grace.

Noah found Grace and therefore he did all that God commanded him.
Noah found Grace and so he listened to what God was saying. Hebrews 11:7.
Noah found Grace and therefore he walked with God. Genesis 6:9
Noah found Grace and therefore he gave thanks to God. Genesis 8:20.

When Noah learned of God's Grace Space his life changed dramatically. Knowledge of the Grace of God just affects the way we live. When Noah learned that the earth was to be destroyed, but he could be saved, it changed everything. And so it should be with us, the simple provision of a Grace Space should shape the way we live. Grace is not a freedom to live however we choose. Grace is a constraint to live a life pleasing to the God who saves us.

For the love of Christ compels us, because we judge thus: that if One died for all, then all died; and He died for all, that those who live should live no longer for themselves, but for Him who died for them and rose again. 2 Corinthians 5: 14-15.

Paul is saying he is convinced that Christ died for all, and that is the same as saying that all have died to sin. When Jesus died, he achieved a Grace Space spacious and strong enough for everyone, even though everyone will not enter it. But because of this provision he and those who believe are constrained by Grace to live a godly life.

Grace to Noah was the ability to stand in relationship with God although all around him were refusing to do so.

Ruth. *Book of Ruth 1-4*

Living in the Favour of God

The story of Ruth is one of the most complete and beautiful stories in the Bible. It is a story of Grace. I encourage you to read the whole thing through in one sitting.

Briefly, there was a famine in the Land of Israel. The famine was always seen as a form of Divine judgement on the people because of disobedience. It was meant as a wake-up call to change direction. The family of Elimelech decided that they weren't taking any of this Divine chastisement stuff, so opted out of the famine and went to live in Moab. They ran away from God. By so doing they stepped out from the Grace of God.

Tragedy strikes the family in Moab, Elimelech, Mahlon and Chilion die and the ageing Naomi is left with her two daughters in law who are Moabitesses. Naomi learns that a time of the Favour of God has returned to the people of Israel and the famine is past, so she decides to go back home to the place of Grace.

1:7. *'She set out on the road that would take them back to the land of Judah.'*

This is the first thing we learn in this story about Divine favour; there is a road back home. Wherever you have been; however long you have been there; whatever the reason you left; whatever you have done; whoever you have been with; whoever you worshipped, whoever you married; no matter what happened to you; no matter what you have said; no matter how old you are; no matter who is now with you – there's a road back home. That is Grace.

If you thought it was God's fault; if you thought it was someone else's fault; or even if you admit it was your fault – there's a road back home. No matter what you dug your heels in about; whom you offended or who offended you; how embarrassing it is; how shameful you feel; how many false starts you have made – there's a road back home. That is Grace.

If there is any purpose in the tragedy and trauma of Moab it was to empty Naomi of her self-sufficiency and cause her to depend entirely on the Favour of God. We need to lay down our self-sufficiency, status, intelligence, learning and personality and step out in faith believing that the favour of God will cover us once again.

As for Ruth, it was her determination to live a life under the canopy of the Grace of God, of which she knew little more than that it was there. These have to be the most beautiful words ever written in all literature:

> *Entreat me not to leave you, or to turn back from following after you; for wherever you go, I will go; and wherever you lodge, I will lodge; your people shall be my people, and your God, my God.* Ruth 1:16.

Naomi and Ruth returned home to Bethlehem. We see how, what appears to happenstance, actually being the Favour of God. She 'just happens' to go to the field of Boaz. He 'just happens' to come along at that moment. Boaz has heard that she has accompanied the ageing Naomi home and her virtue has been noted. Immediately she becomes the recipient of Divine Favour. Not only can she collect the dropped stalks, she is placed under protection and the harvesters are commanded to deliberately drop a few more stalks of grain for her and at the end of the day she is given part of the harvest to take home. Grace from our viewpoint often looks like happenstance, but actually it is the hand of God.

But we need to note how Ruth was addressed. 'Ruth the Moabitess.' Now this was not polite, in fact it was an insult. Deuteronomy 23:3 says

'No Moabite may enter the assembly of the Lord down to the 10th generation.'

We know where the story is going, she moves on from the favour of the farmer to marrying him and bearing children who become ancestors of King David, and later on, Jesus the Messiah. In Old Testament terms there could be no greater honour, yet she remains Ruth the Moabitess.

Another law was in force. Isaiah 56: 1-8.

let no foreigner who has joined himself to the Lord say the Lord will surely exclude me from his people.......and foreigners who bind themselves to the Lord to serve him, to love the Name of the Lord and to worship him.....these will I bring to my Holy Mountain and give them joy in my house of prayer..... for my house will be called a house of prayer for all nations.

It shows us that Divine Favour takes the despised, the stranger and the foreigner and makes them part of the royal family of Israel. God doesn't shine up our past, he doesn't pretend it didn't happen or wasn't important; he transforms what was once a stigma into a badge of honour. The wonder is in the Favour of God that has the power to transform lives. Not to remind the person of who they were, but to display to the world the things God can do with a life that comes to him empty and humble, blaming no one but themselves for their tragedy; aware that God has taken the tragedy they caused and turned it into stepping stones back to a right relationship with God.

- The redeemer is not afraid of difficult and complex situations.
- The redeemer is willing and able to redeem
- The redeemer was there all the time.
- The redeemer was waiting to be asked.

When we first step into God's favour it is like Ruth gleaning. We just pick up what is left lying around. It's nothing complicated like the sermon or the key of the music or the layout of the building; it's the greeting, it's who speaks to me and how, it's the atmosphere, its being left alone just to pick up the stalks for a while. Ruth was spoken to graciously. She was a stranger, but she was treated as if she belonged.

The story ends with the outline of the family down to King David. Ruth became an ancestor of the Kings of Israel, and as we know from the New Testament, King David was an ancestor of Jesus the Messiah. You have been called to dwell under Divine Favour so that Divine Favour can encompass others. Ruth could never have dreamed of what God would bring about through her appeal to the Kinsman Redeemer that night at the threshing floor.

To summarise:

There will always be a road back into a state of Grace.

The redeemer will always be waiting for us to come.
What seems like good fortune is actually the Grace of God.
His Grace is shown to the undeserving.
His Grace turns a stigma of shame into a badge of honour.
He places us in the centre of his plans and purposes.

David *1 Samuel 16-1 Kings 2.*

Grace bringing forgiveness

The story of the life of David is one of the most exhaustive in the entire Bible. However, on the subject of Grace, it is the matter of Bathsheba, the wife of Uriah the Hittite, that is most pertinent.

The historic story is told in 2 Samuel 11-12, but the most poignant reflections are found in the Psalms. David saw Bathsheba leaving a *Miqveh* [101] after her ritual purification. (2 Samuel 11:4) He desired her and sent for her. She became pregnant. David then sets about trying to cover it all up. Firstly, by trying to get Uriah, Bathsheba's husband to sleep with his own wife so it would seem he was the father of the child. He tried again by making Uriah drunk, but he still did not go to his wife. Finally, he ordered the military commander to put Uriah in the most dangerous place in the on-going battle so that he would not survive. Uriah was killed in battle. After a time of mourning, Bathsheba was brought to David's palace and became his wife.

> And when her mourning was over, David sent and brought her to his house, and she became his wife and bore him a son. But the thing that David had done displeased the Lord.

---

[101] A ritual bath where women who purify themselves after their period. They would immerse themselves in the water fully clothed.

2 Samuel 11:27.

Bathsheba became David's eighth official wife,[102] he had many more concubines. These actions took David beyond the authority he had as King. Deuteronomy 17:17. He was exercising a liberty he had no right to. As such he stepped out of the place of Grace that God had provided for him. His actions caused chaos for himself and for others. The Lord sends Nathan the prophet to David with a solemn message:

> I gave you your master's house and your master's wives into your keeping, and gave you the house of Israel and Judah. And if that had been too little, I also would have given you much more! Why have you despised the commandment of the Lord, to do evil in His sight? You have killed Uriah the Hittite with the sword; you have taken his wife to be your wife, and have killed him with the sword of the people of Ammon. Now therefore, the sword shall never depart from your house, because you have despised Me, and have taken the wife of Uriah the Hittite to be your wife.' Thus says the Lord: "Behold, I will raise up adversity against you from your own house; and I will take your wives before your eyes and give them to your neighbour, and he shall lie with your wives in the sight of this sun. For you did it secretly, but I will do this thing before all Israel, before the sun." So, David said to Nathan, "I have sinned against the Lord." And Nathan said to David, "The Lord also has put away your sin; you shall not die. However, because by this deed you have given great occasion to the enemies of the Lord to blaspheme, the child also who is born to you shall surely die." Then Nathan departed to his house. 2 Samuel. 8-15

Although David would be restored, the consequences of his actions would unfold, despite his pleading with the Lord for it to be otherwise. He had unleashed violent jealousy and a desire for vengeance that would not be silenced over generations. Grief would strike his own heart because the

---

[102] 1 Samuel 18:27; 1 Samuel 25:39-42; 1 Samuel 25:43; 2 Samuel 3:2-5; 1 Chronicles 14:3-5.

child would die. David's sin demanded death. Grace will save the sinner from God's wrath, when the sinner repents, but it may not arrest the course of evil that has been set in motion. This is an amazing picture of the mixture of justice and mercy.

Yet this description only scratches the surface regarding what went on in David's heart as a result of his action. We need to turn to the Psalms to discover more. It is a clear picture of the depravity of human nature. Where sin reigned, death reigned and chaos unfolded. But is also a picture of Grace. Where sin reigned and death reigned and chaos ensued, Grace abounded more! Even though a chaotic stream of events was set in motion, there would be redemption for anyone who called upon the name of the Lord. Even Bathsheba was redeemed by becoming the mother of Solomon, the next king of Israel.

Grace abandoned.

David fell from Grace because he failed to keep God's laws. David thought that as he was the chosen king, he didn't have to keep the laws if they were inconvenient. I remember as a child we used to sing a song that contained the lines:

I am not under law, I'm under grace,
It was grace that rescued me, it was grace that set me free;
I have sought, I have found a hiding place,
I am not under law, I'm under grace. [103]

At face value, it carries the sentiment that we are free from the regulations of the sacrificial laws of Israel. There is nothing we need to do to gain salvation except believe. That is true, but most of us were never under the sacrificial laws of Israel in the first place. It has been taken to mean, in some circles, that it doesn't really matter how I conduct my

---

[103] C A Miles 1868-1946.

business, relationships, and responsibilities. Grace is a giant safety net, so that whenever I fall off the wire, I will be okay. Everything will be okay. Being under Grace does not mean we can neglect the laws of God. This was the case for David and it is the case for us as well. Grace enables me to uphold the law of God.

A young lady came into a church I was leading and gave her life to Christ. She was a brand-new convert, never been to church before. She began to grow in faith and was baptised. After some time, she had to go on a conference for a few days for her work. While she was there she slept with someone and became pregnant. Of course, the secret was soon obvious. She tried to take her life, unsuccessfully, thankfully. But I never forget what she said to me, '*I thought that now I was a Christian God would look after me and I wouldn't become pregnant.*'

> *What shall we say then? Shall we continue in sin that grace may abound? Certainly not! How shall we who died to sin live any longer in it?* Romans 6:1-2.

Christianity is not a religion without sacrifice. Just because we don't take a lamb to church every Sunday to be sacrificed, does not mean we are without blood sacrifice. I don't mean spiritual sacrifices. We have a blood sacrifice. One. Once for all forever. Jesus. All the sacrifices of the Old Testament that covered sin are represented in what Jesus did. But we still are expected not to murder, commit adultery and covet our neighbours' goods.

The difference is that we do not refrain from these things to tick things off on a list to score points with God; we do them, or don't do them as the case may be, out of gratitude to Jesus for dying for us to provide a place of Grace wherein we can stand. We have an inner motivation to do the will of God.

Grace is primarily a place where we *stand* not where we *fall*. The goal of the Law was to produce holiness. The goal of Grace is to produce holiness. Some religions compel its adherents by fear of failure, as we have seen. But the word of God establishes obedience out of *Gratitude*. We are to be so grateful for Grace that we will not do anything to offend the Lord Jesus.

Grace sought after.

David knew all that, but he sinned anyway. What do we do in that case? Realise that what we have done was part of the wounds that our saviour bore. And it was unnecessary pain! He had already suffered sufficiently to save us! So, like David, we must repent. There is sufficient Grace to return, but we have wounded the Saviour.

David was saved from his sin because he heard the word of the Lord and he sought forgiveness. But it was an agonising process. He realised there was nothing he could do to obtain restitution. He couldn't bring Uriah back to life or reverse the pregnancy. But he could cry for mercy.

But if we dare to think of Grace as an easy option, we need to consider Psalm 6. We see the precarious spiritual state of someone who has fallen from a place of standing in Grace. David went into the house of God. He met directly with God. No priest. No sacrifice. Although they were available. A man and God face to face. This does not preclude sharing things with believers whom we trust, but it does show that ultimately it is a matter between man and God. '*Against You, You only, have I sinned!*'

> *O Lord, do not rebuke me in Your anger, nor chasten me in Your hot displeasure. Have mercy on me, O Lord, for I am weak; O Lord, heal me, for my bones are troubled. My soul also is*

greatly troubled; but You, O Lord—how long? Return, O Lord, deliver me! Oh, save me for Your mercies' sake! For in death there is no remembrance of You; in the grave who will give You thanks? I am weary with my groaning; all night I make my bed swim; I drench my couch with my tears. My eye wastes away because of grief; it grows old because of all my enemies. Psalm 6.

O Lord, do not rebuke me in Your wrath, nor chasten me in Your hot displeasure! For Your arrows pierce me deeply, and Your hand presses me down. There is no soundness in my flesh because of Your anger, nor any health in my bones because of my sin. For my iniquities have gone over my head; like a heavy burden they are too heavy for me. My wounds are foul and festering because of my foolishness. I am troubled, I am bowed down greatly; I go mourning all the day long. For my loins are full of inflammation, and there is no soundness in my flesh. I am feeble and severely broken; I groan because of the turmoil of my heart. Psalm 38:1-8.

If we open our heart in penitence, the 'Chastening of the Lord' is more painful, more appropriate, and more life-changing, than any strictures a human priest can prescribe. David headed off down the road he had chosen. But God placed a Grace Space in his path so he could be restored.

Grace found.

Then you will call upon Me and go and pray to Me, and I will listen to you. And you will seek Me and find Me, when you search for Me with all your heart. I will be found by you, says the Lord, and I will bring you back from your captivity. Jeremiah 29:12-14.

This is what I've learned through it all: all believers should confess their sins to God; do it every time God has uncovered you in the time of exposing. For if you do this, when sudden storms of life overwhelm, you'll be kept safe. Lord, you are my

secret hiding place, protecting me from these troubles, surrounding me with songs of gladness! Your joyous shouts of rescue release my breakthrough.
Psalm 32:6-7. The Passion Translation.

Grace is not illusive. God says that he will be found. David set out on an 'experimental' journey. We have mentioned that he did not seek a priest. He did not bring a sacrifice. He did not ask for the 'ephod' as in days gone by. He considered the enormity of his sin beyond the scope of what a priest and a sacrifice could atone for. If there was any hope for him it would be a matter between him and God. He would approach God on the basis of the Word of the Lord that has been spoken by Nathan, '*the Lord has put away your sin.*'

So, he did, without precedent or reference, he threw himself on the mercies of God. In so doing he found Grace. So impacting was his experience that he set up a new way of worship for the remainder of his lifetime. There would be no regular sacrifices in the tabernacle he had erected to house the Ark. Psalm 51:17-17. The priests would be sent to Gibeon, where Moses' Tabernacle was, to perform the sacrifices. 1 Chronicles 16: 39. But the people would be encouraged to seek the Lord directly as he had done.

We can conclude this section with the words of the greatest of the Penitentiary Psalms, Psalm 51.

Purify my conscience! Make this leper clean again! Wash me in your love until I am pure in heart. Satisfy me in your sweetness, and my song of joy will return. The places you have crushed within me will rejoice in your healing touch. Hide my sins from your face; erase all my guilt by your saving grace. Keep creating in me a clean heart.
Fill me with pure thoughts and holy desires, ready to please you. May you never reject me! May you never take from me your sacred Spirit! Let my passion for life be restored, tasting joy in every breakthrough you bring to me. Hold me close to you with

a willing spirit that obeys whatever you say. Then I can show other guilty ones how loving and merciful you are. They will find their way back home to you, knowing that you will forgive them. O God, my saving God deliver me fully from every sin, even the sin that brought bloodguilt. Then my heart will once again be thrilled to sing the passionate songs of joy and deliverance! [104]

Esther. *The Book of Esther 1-10.*

Grace: the only hope.

They keyword in the story of Esther is the word '*Favour.*' 'She found favour in the king's sight.' Esther 5:2. Favour, as we know is an equivalent word for Grace. This is Grace; the only hope. As Ruth 1:16, to me, is the finest verse in all literature, then the following verse is a close second.

> "*And so, I will go to the king, which is against the law; and if I perish, I perish!*" Esther 4:16.

Like the book of Ruth, you need to read the whole book of Esther to get the picture of what was going on in this story.

Briefly, the story is set in Shushan, Susa today, in Iran. The story begins with the deposition of the Queen Vashti, the wife of Ahasuerus. In order to replace her a 'beauty contest' is held. Esther comes out in favour and is crowned the Queen. Esther is a Jewess, a descendant of the Babylonian captives. But no one knows this yet.

The king's second in command is a man called Haman. He hated the Jews and even more so now Esther is Queen. He tricks the king into passing a law that says on a certain date

---

[104] The Passion Translation

the Jews can be exterminated. Esther has an uncle called Mordecai. He gets the message to Esther about what is planned and urges her to go to the king and get the law repealed, otherwise she, and all the Jews will die.

Esther has a few difficulties.
1. She cannot enter the presence of the king unless she is summoned, on pain of death.
2. If she does venture into his presence, her only hope is that he holds out a golden sceptre to her as sign she has been accepted or favoured. 4:11.
3. She has not been summoned into the king's presence for 30 days, so she knows she is not the flavour of the month.
4. She realises however that she is where she is for this precise purpose. 4:13-14.

So, we return to the verse we quoted at the beginning. *"I will go into the king and if I perish, I perish."*

There are several ways the details of this story can be applied as illustrations of the gospel, and probably the parallel I am drawing is not the best of them. Be that as it may we will proceed. What is clear is that the only hope for the Jewish community was that she finds *Favour* with the king. She had found favour before 2:17; but she was not favourite at present. This illustrates the scenario when there is nothing to be done except an act of Grace.

Esther enters the king's court and the sceptre is extended, she is accepted. To quickly wrap up the story, Haman is executed, Mordecai is promoted, and the Jews are saved.

Salvation comes about because there is nothing left to hope for except Grace. All the comments and quotes we have made about depravity come into focus. We are not righteous or worthy to come into God's presence. Sin has separated us from God. If his holiness and our sinfulness should come into contact, we would perish. Everything comes down to Grace.

Two things come into focus;

The Holiness of God.

We have come to the place where we need to emphasise the Holiness of God. Holiness is God's moral quality. We need to fix our minds for a moment or two on his sheer purity, transparency, and righteousness. Our vision of the Lord is of a God, as much **not** like ourselves, as it is possible to be.

> *In the year that King Uzziah died, I saw the Lord sitting on a throne, high and lifted up, and the train of His robe filled the temple. Above it stood seraphim; each one had six wings: with two he covered his face, with two he covered his feet, and with two he flew. And one cried to another and said:*
> *"Holy, holy, holy is the Lord of hosts; the whole earth is full of His glory!"* Isaiah 6: 1-3.

Unto the Son He says, Your throne, O God, is forever and ever; A sceptre of righteousness is the sceptre of Your kingdom. You have loved righteousness and hated lawlessness; Therefore God, Your God, has anointed You With the oil of gladness more than Your companions.
Hebrews 1: 8-9

The use of a rod or staff as a symbol of authority stretches back to the beginning of time. It was originally thought to have developed from a shepherd's staff. As time went by, they were covered in gold and jewels. The British monarchy still uses a sceptre for state occasions. The sceptre of Ahasuerus signified his absolute power and sovereignty. He could do as he wished. In his kingdom his laws are irrevocable. He could pronounce death; he could pronounce life. He could promote; he could demote. He could accept; he could reject. He loved what he loved; he hated what he hated. No one could approach him unless he desired them to do so. And he had no need to ask anyone's advice. He was a despot, but as such he was an antitype of the Holiness and Sovereignty of God. God's sceptre signifies the same things.

The Sinfulness of Mankind.

Esther was required to step into the presence of a man such as this, a man who remember, had just signed her death warrant.

> *And there is no creature hidden from His sight, but all things are naked and open to the eyes of Him to whom we must give account.* Hebrews 4:13.

> *For the wrath of God is revealed from heaven against all ungodliness and unrighteousness of men, who suppress the truth in unrighteousness.* Romans 1:18.

> *As it is written: There is none righteous, no, not one; there is none who understands; there is none who seeks after God. They have all turned aside; They have together become unprofitable; there is none who does good, no, not one. Their throat is an open tomb; with their tongues they have practiced deceit; The poison of asps is under their lips, whose mouth is full of cursing and bitterness......the way of peace they have not known. Their feet are swift to shed blood; destruction and misery are in no fear of God before their eyes.* Romans 3:10-18.

> *For our God is a consuming fire. Hebrews 12:29.*

Ahasuerus, despite being a despot and a tyrant, had a provision in his court ritual where, if he chose, he could grant favour to someone other than himself. The sub-title of this book is, *'Where the sheer holiness of God and the sinfulness of man meet, and we are not consumed.'*

God has determined to offer Grace to those who approach

him in humility and repentance. To 'touch the sceptre' is to acknowledge the Sovereignty of God. He can, in fact, do as he pleases without any concern for us. It is to acknowledge that we are helpless in our sin and only the redeeming Grace of God can save us. It is to acknowledge that the pathway of salvation is nothing of our doing, but a provision God has laid down for me to step into.

As with Esther, the situation had got to the point with mankind where there was nothing else to be hoped for except favour.

> *And the posts of the door were shaken by the voice of him who cried out, and the house was filled with smoke. So I said: "Woe is me, for I am undone! Because I am a man of unclean lips, and I dwell in the midst of a people of unclean lips; for my eyes have seen the King the Lord of hosts." Then one of the seraphim flew to me, having in his hand a live coal which he had taken with the tongs from the altar. And he touched my mouth with it, and said: "Behold, this has touched your lips; Your iniquity is taken away, and your sin purged."* Isaiah 6:4-7.

There is a Divine exchange in the Grace Space. Unworthiness for worthiness; rejection for acceptance; sinful to holy; the sentence of death to the privilege of life.

Paul. *Acts 7-28.*

Transforming Grace

> *For I am the least of the apostles, who am not worthy to be called an apostle, because I persecuted the church of God. But by the grace of God, I am what I am, and His grace toward me was not in vain; but I laboured more abundantly than they all, yet not I, but the grace of God which was with me.*
> 1 Corinthians 15: 9-10.

Any discussion regarding Paul and Grace must start with these famous words, '*I am what I am by the Grace of the Lord.*'

There was a lot of scepticism about Paul. Not everyone liked him or trusted him. He was the first believer to have previously been a persecutor of the church. He presents himself here as a late-comer to the ministry and considers himself the least worthy of the founding apostles. However, he does consider his vision of the risen Christ equivalent to the post resurrection appearances of Jesus to the other apostles and brothers.

He then says that all the witnesses of the resurrection have preached the gospel of the risen saviour, just the same as he has. The message is the same whether you are listening to one of them or to Paul. Paul's claim is that he stands among this hallowed throng by the Grace of God alone.

Here we are looking at Grace that qualifies a person for Holy Office. Paul frequently gives us a veiled glimpse of his inadequacies. His being born out of time. he may well have had a vision of Jesus, but he had not walked with him as the others had done.

Galatians 6:11.
Maybe this is a reference to poor eyesight.

2 Corinthians 10:10.
He seems to have had some kind of physical ailment.

1 Corinthians 2:3-4.
He seemed to have initially approached the task of the ministry in much apprehension and his words were nervously uttered.

He admits in 2 Corinthians 11: 6 that he was not an eloquent speaker.

2 Corinthians 12:7. He again discloses some form of physical ailment that constantly bothered him.

Paul's confession amounted to three things; he felt he was unworthy; unable; and unqualified.
Paul's conclusion to all this is not that he is unsuitable for the ministry, but that he can only function as an apostle by the Grace of God. 1 Corinthians 1:26.

This is for people who feel the call of God on their life but are overwhelmed by their own inadequacies.

Paul found that the Grace of God enabled him to receive and communicate things from God to man. Ephesians 3:3-7. If God is revealing things to you, and those around you confirm that what you have is from God, then seek an outlet for what you have received. In Paul's day it was confined to preaching and writing. These methods are still available, but the electronic world has opened many new avenues of communication.

Paul found the Grace that called him also equipped him. 1 Corinthians 12:10.
He received the physical metabolism to withstand perilous times. 2 Corinthians 11:24-27. He received the aptitude to confront hostile crowds. Acts 21:40. The wisdom to address those of other religions. Acts 17:22. And the integrity to offer advice on the basis of things God had shown to him. Acts 27:10; 23-24. He was able to take the advice not to face the mob in Ephesus. Acts 19: 30.

Paul found the Grace of God was quite sufficient for him. 2 Corinthians 12:9.
At times when he could not foresee what to do, God would

place someone across his path to encourage and direct him. The believers in Damascus. 12 Corinthians 11:32-33; his nephew who uncovered a plotted assassination. Acts 23:16. Timothy was there to see to some practical things. 2 Timothy 4:13; Paul was assured that the Grace of God would enable him to accomplish the task he had been called to accomplish. 2 Timothy 4: 17-18.

Paul found that he had been given *authority by God to bring the gospel of Grace to the gentiles.*[105] Ephesians 3:2. This in itself was a controversial matter. There were those who felt the gospel should not go to the gentiles, as Peter had found out earlier. Acts 11:3; 15:1. Although Peter had gone to Cornelius and defended his ministry, he was obviously pressurised about his views. Galatians 2:11-12.

Paul ignored the dissenters in a way Peter had not done up to this point. Grace has authority. When that Grace has been recognised in you by those who have leadership, then let nothing stop you from the calling God has given you. Galatians 2:7-10.

From then on, in every one of his letters Paul begins by saying, Grace and Peace, or Grace Mercy and Peace, be to you. In other words, why am I writing to you; what authority do I have; and how do you know what I am saying is from God? The answer is the Grace that God has given to me.

The will of God will never take you,
Where the grace of God cannot keep you.
Where the arms of God cannot support you,
Where the riches of God cannot supply your needs,
Where the power of God cannot endow you.

The will of God will never take you,

---

[105] The Dispensation of Grace given to me. KJV.

Where the spirit of God cannot work through you,
Where the wisdom of God cannot teach you,
Where the army of God cannot protect you,
Where the hands of God cannot mould you.

The will of God will never take you,
Where the love of God cannot enfold you,
Where the mercies of God cannot sustain you,
Where the peace of God cannot calm your fears,
Where the authority of God cannot overrule for you.

The will of God will never take you,
Where the comfort of God cannot dry your tears,
Where the Word of God cannot feed you,
Where the miracles of God cannot be done for you,
Where the omnipresence of God cannot find you.[106]

What have we discovered about the dimensions of Grace? Noah saw a Gracious God from the depths of human depravity. Ruth set out to find the Grace she had only heard of and found it in her future. David found Grace that reached deep within to cleanse from the guilt of sin. Esther was convinced the only hope was Grace, so she risked all to find it. Paul stepped into Grace and was transformed from an enemy of the Gospel into its greatest exponent.

---

[106] Anon.

The Grace Space

CHAPTER TWELVE.

The Triumphs of Grace

In his triumphal hymn, *O for a Thousand Tongues to sing*, Charles Wesley closes his first verse with this phrase. '*The triumphs of his Grace.*' When sung to the tune 'Lyngham' the line is repeated 3 times, emphasising the life-changing power of the Grace of God. In this chapter I have tried to illustrate this by selecting five true stories where Grace triumphed. Wesley's fourth verse emphasises this.

> *He breaks the power of cancelled sin*
> *He sets the prisoner free*
> *His blood can make the foulest clean*
> *His blood avails for me.*

We shall see the triumph of Grace where it would humanly be expected that Grace would never be found, but it was. The theme of the bible is, 'Grace is found where it is not expected to be.' If anything, this chapter will enforce the significance of the '*undeserving.*'

The critics are right: Grace is unfair. We deserve God's wrath and get God's love, deserve punishment and get forgiveness. We don't get what we deserve. Paul put it ironically, The wages of sin is death, the gift of God is eternal life. We work hard for wages, which vanish at death; we do nothing to deserve grace, and get life eternal. If you want fairness, try a religion like Hinduism, which says we may have to go through thousands, even millions of incarnations before paying for all our sins. It's unfair that a human rights abuser like Saul gets forgiven, or a murderer/adulterer like King David, or a thief hanging on a cross who has a conversion just before death. Yes, it's unfair—gloriously unfair I would say.[107]

In regard to Israel the bible makes it clear that the nation would be restored in the last days in preparation for her salvation at the appearing of the Messiah. God would again show Grace to the descendants of Abraham. But this display of Grace would scandalise the nations of the world so much they would seek to destroy Israel. But God will defend her. Zechariah 12:1-9.

We live in the time where it is politically fashionable to denounce Israel as occupiers, colonists, racists, and a threat to world peace. Even in the church there are significant numbers who would agree and see no place for Israel as a nation. They would say everything that was once belonging to Israel as far as her relationship with God is concerned, now belongs to the church. But God has promised to show Grace again to the descendants of Abraham in their land. This be-fuddles the intellect. Zechariah 12:2. It is impossible to change. Zechariah 12:3. It scrambles the plans of the aggressor. Zechariah 12:4. They that seek to destroy Israel will be destroyed themselves in the process. Zechariah 12:6.

And I will pour on the house of David and on the inhabitants of Jerusalem the Spirit of grace and supplication; then they

---

[107] Philip Yancey.

will look on Me whom they pierced. Yes, they will mourn for Him as one mourns for his only son, and grieve for Him as one grieves for a firstborn. Zechariah 12:10.

God pours out his Grace where we least expect it, where we cannot reconcile it with our concepts of justice and fairness, and where we may think it is thoroughly undeserved. But because it is '*undeserved favour'* is that not what we should be expecting?

> *Moreover, the law entered that the offense might abound. But where sin abounded, grace abounded much more,* Romans 5:20.

I have selected historical situations where incredible Grace was demonstrated against the backdrop of terrible sin. There are countless such stories. I have selected ones that have particularly impacted me. The stories have come from the people I have met, the places I have been, and information that has come my way. Dates and names have been taken from publications and online sites.

This chapter teaches us that no circumstances are too far gone, and no person is so depraved, that the Grace of God cannot reach them. Some theologians speak of the '*Scandal of Grace.*' Hillsong United have published a song with this as the title.

> *Grace what have You done murdered for me on that cross*
> *Accused in absence of wrong*
> *my sin washed away in Your blood*
> *Too much to make sense of it all*
> *I know that Your love breaks my fall*
> *The scandal of grace*
> *You died in my place so my soul will live.* [108]

---

[108] Words and Music by Matt Crocker & Joel Houston

The Scandal of Grace is a demonstration of Grace, operating in the space where, humanly speaking, everyone has walked away and even angels have bowed their heads and folded their wings and given up. (1Peter 1:12) It is when the powerful virtues of justice and righteousness are overruled and scandalised by the higher power of Grace.

In no way should these stories, as I have written them, be read as a historical or biographical accounts. The only reason names, dates, and a historical sequence has been quoted is to paint a background picture of where God's amazing Grace was manifested. In fact, I have tried to only refer to articles that were written from a similar perspective. I am fascinated by history, I read about historical events, but I am not a historian. I do not feel adequate to interpret history and assess the emotions present in the situations I have presented. Be careful if you quote from these pages to support historical events, because although I have been careful about the details, there may still be variations. These are articles about Grace not about history or biography. They are presented to display the Greatness of God's Grace not the wickedness or frailty of man. They are written that we may draw the conclusion, if God could have done that then, in those circumstances, with those people, then there is no circumstance under heaven that I may find myself in that God's grace cannot penetrate.

Scandalous Grace.

Captain Henry Gerecke U.S. Army Chaplain.

If there was ever a time and a place on earth where one would have thought it impossible to find a strand of Grace it would have been from the 20th of November 1945 to the 1st of October 1946 in the city of Nuremberg, Germany. It was the time of the International Military Tribunal where the surviving leaders of Nazi Germany were tried. But it was not the case. Amazingly a Grace Space was carved out in the midst of the accounts of the atrocities unprecedented in human history on such a scale. A Grace Space so unbelievable, that even today when we read about it, there is a feeling that even God contradicted himself and went soft on justice. Actually, it was a time where God's Great Grace appeared to shine brighter than the midday sun against the utter blackness of the setting where it happened.

This aspect of Grace, as far as I can see, has never been highlighted in the historic films or documentaries of the trial. It is the subject of a few books but somehow it remains obscure in the annals of history. However, there are several short articles available on the internet that makes it difficult to attribute the information to one particular source. [109]

The man of God in question was Captain Henry Gerecke of the United States Army Chaplaincy Corps. He was a German speaking Evangelical Lutheran Pastor who firmly believed in the need for personal repentance and acceptance of Jesus Christ as Lord and Saviour. He was appointed Chaplain to the 21 protestant Nazi leaders on trial at Nuremberg.

The story has already been told but it deserves to be retold, again and again, to every generation, for two important reasons. The first has to do with the men to whom he ministered, the ones who repented and believed in Christ. The scandal of Christianity is not that these men went to heaven; it is that God loved them so much that he was willing to die to get them there. Had it been a human decision, many would have thrown these men, guilty of such atrocities, into the

---

[109] The dates and finer details are taken from works by Chad Bird, Tim Townsend, and Railton and by Henry Gerecke himself.

flames of hell. [110]

On the basis of that comment, I feel entitled to tell the story again in this context.

Single-handedly, under the anointing of the Holy Spirit, Gerecke pushed back on one side the mountain of atrocities evident in the bodies of what would amount to over 6 million Jewish people; thousands of Romany people, who knows how many disabled people, plus countless millions that had died in battle, and on the other side the anger, hatred and utter outrage of the rest of humanity, and the righteous anger of God, and established a Grace Space where men found Christ as their Saviour.

He saw it as, *'A battle for the souls of men standing beneath the shadow of the Gallows.'* [111] Gerecke never minimised the atrocities, or sought to soften the guilt, but held firmly to the belief that God was the ultimate judge of all and it was his solemn duty to lead, whoever would come, to the foot of the cross.

Of the 21 men entrusted to him, 13 accepted his ministry, and of those, 8 came to faith in Jesus Christ. They were, Field Marshall Wilhelm Keitel, Field Marshall Joachim von Ribbentrop, Field Marshall Albert Kesselring, [112] Obergruppenfuhrer Fritz Saukel, Admiral Erich Raeder, Reichminister Albert Speer, Reichsleiter Baldur von Schirach, and Ministerialdirektor Hans Fritzsche. They and their subordinates had committed the most horrendous crimes which are well documented elsewhere.
Of these men, Ribbentrop, Keitel, and Saukel were hanged.

---

[110] From Hitlers Wolves to Christs Lambs. Chad Bird.
[111] Hans Frietzche acquitted prisoner.
[112] Kesselring was a witness at Nuremberg not an accused. He was tried later in Venice.

Fritzsche and Schacht were declared not guilty, the others received lengthy imprisonments.

Gerecke was charged with 'easy grace.' In fact, he received many abusive letters from people whose view of Grace was abjectly inadequate. How could he determine the genuineness of the confessions and repentance of these men? Even if they were genuine, how could God forgive what they had done? Gerecke gave each of his communicants the same charge.

> *I now ask you before God, is this your sincere confession, that you heartily repent of your sins, believe on Jesus Christ, and sincerely and earnestly purpose, by the assistance of God the Holy Spirit, from now on to amend your sinful life? Then declare so by saying: 'Yes.'*

The prison guards were so touched by what we today would call '*the presence of the Holy Spirit,*' that they left Gerecke alone, locked in the chapel with men who only a few months previously were directing atrocities. They are apparently reported as saying, '*This is holy business.*'

The fact was that Gerecke was well experienced in dealing with prisoners and the deviousness they often presented. He was also fluent in German. These were the reasons he was chosen for the job. He held services with the men every Sunday for approximately 9 months. In addition, he constantly held private conversations with each of the prisoners whether they were open to faith or not. He knew them and their families more intimately than anyone else on earth. He was not easily deceived and was very careful about whom he admitted to the sacred act of Holy Communion. In fact, he refused Goering because of the insincerity of his approach to faith and God. Others went to their death disinterested. Gerecke was inspired by these words:

The Grace Space

Lord lay some soul upon my heart
And love that soul through me;
And may I nobly do my part
To win that soul for Thee.

And when I come to the beautiful city
And the saved all from around me appear,
I want to hear somebody tell me
It was you who invited me here.[113]

It is most unlikely that anyone reading these words will ever find themselves in a place like Henry Gerecke found himself. However, situations that are far less dramatic by comparison can be equally as traumatic to the persons involved. Be encouraged and strengthened that God's Grace has no boundaries and there is no situation it cannot transform.

If someone is reading this book and you are the perpetrator of some horrendous deed and are racked with guilt and shame, please know that you are not beyond the reach of God's Boundless Grace. There is room at the cross for you.

On the other hand, if you may be someone who is a victim of some horrendous deed and find it difficult to forgive and move on, may the same Grace fill your heart and heal your wounds. Your resentment does not hold the perpetrator in a prison, it holds you in a prison. You are locked in with the horrors of the incident you are trying to forget. Let faith arise in our hearts to the God who will judge wisely and fairly and will deliver a verdict where all the supreme virtues of justice, righteousness, humility, grace and mercy are marvellously entwined together.

By telling this story I am not minimising the horror of the holocaust or other atrocities that have been committed of a similar nature. There are other such stories, but I leave them

---

[113] A hymn by B B McKinney that inspired Gerecke.

for someone else to tell. It is simply that this story has touched my heart, and I hope it will touch yours also.

But he who is spiritual appraises all things, yet he himself is appraised by no one. 1 Corinthians 2:15.

He is the Rock! His work is perfect,
For all His ways are just;
A God of truth and without injustice,
Righteous and upright is He.
Deuteronomy 32:4

Persistent Grace

Washington Okumu.

Washington Okumu was born in Kenya in 1936. He died in 2016. He was educated in a number of institutions including Harvard and Cambridge. He eventually worked for the Kenyan government and became recognised as a diplomat. As far as political figures go, Okumu is relatively unknown. But God had a job for him to do, so profoundly important, that it changed the course of history.

I first need to paint he background picture. The year was 1994. The place was the Republic of South Africa. The occasion was the first universal-franchise democratic elections. Frederick Willem de Klerk was the president. He had bravely turned his back on apartheid and white supremacy and set out on the precarious journey to universal franchise. He was right, but not everyone agreed. Powerful forces would kill to have their way, and they did!

By this time South Africa was in a state of near anarchy. It was considered the most dangerous place to live in the world. The murder rate in the USA was deemed to be 10 per

100,000, in South Africa it was 98 per 100,000. My family and I lived there during this period. Political leaders sat tentatively around conference tables, but the rank and file of groups on the extreme left and right sought to make the country ungovernable.

Tribal loyalties mingled with political aspirations and caused deep, and seemingly, irreconcilable divides. Most notable was the divide between the African National Congress, the largest party, led by the great Nelson Mandela and the Inkatha Freedom Party, the second largest party, led by Mangosuthu Buthelezi, Chief of the formidable Zulu tribe.

Mandela championed a single unitary state while Buthelezi propagated a federal system of independent regions. Unique in political wranglings however, was the fact that all the protagonists were, to some extent or other, God-fearing men. By 'God fearing' I do not mean that they all had an experience of saving faith, but that they acknowledged to supremacy of God and held the Word of God in reverence. Amazingly, in our secular world, often the bitter negotiations began and ended in prayer.

Talks were convened, broken up and convened again. Parties sat down and got up and walked away, and returned again. Tables were thumped, voices were raised, doors were slammed shut, but the glue that held it all together were the prayers of God-fearing people and the practical participation of church leaders and Christian business people.

17th November 1993, the interim constitution is signed.
14th December 1993 the Inkatha Freedom Party representing the Zulu nation decided to boycott any election.
Finally, we arrive at 1994.
18th March 1994. The Zulu king, Goodwill Zwelithini, declares Zululand an independent state and calls upon his people to fight for their freedom. Mangosuthu Buthelezi withdrew from

talks. The elections were set for 27th April. The 80,000,000 voting papers were printed without the Inkatha Freedom Party's name.

Enter God's man. Washington Okumu. He had been a junior aid among the international mediators, but now most of them had left in despair. Christian leaders persuaded Okumu to return to South Africa. A fax was sent to Buthelezi. 'Okumu is coming in the name of the Lord and in his personal capacity.' Okumu met with virtually everybody, but the Zulu divide only deepened. On the 13th April all international mediation finally collapsed.

Buthelezi prepared to leave Johannesburg to return to Zululand to defend his ancestral lands. Washington Okumu set out to speak to him one last time. He went to the wrong airport. He wasn't flying from the international airport but one nearby called Lanseria.

Okumu arrived. Buthelezi's plane was already taxying for take-off. Okumu watched in horror as the plane rose to the sky. It was a declaration of war. But God was at work. In minutes the pilot radioed back to the airport that they had a technical issue and were returning. Okumu was over-joyed, and so was the whole of praying South Africa when we learned of it the following day. I still am moved to tears when I retell the story today.

Okumu and Buthelezi met, a break-through was achieved, the war was defused, the elections went ahead with Inkatha. For several years afterwards, at least as long as Nelson Mandela was alive, South Africa knew relative peace and prosperity.

The faith, tenacity and total devotion of one man, Washington Okumu, carved out a Grace Space. God himself caused a compass to malfunction. All the political and spiritual men of the day had come to the end. Yet through Okumu's devotion to God and the cause of peace, a nation was saved from a blood bath. When the plane was examined, no fault was found. This was an act of God.

Buthelezi went on television in repentance and humility and likened himself to the disobedient prophet Jonah. As God had brought Jonah back to his will by means of the whale, he had been brought back by a malfunctioning compass system and the persistence of the man of God.

We worked day and night for the next 12 days. The polling stations were made ready. 80,000,000 adhesive strips were printed and fixed to the ballot papers to include Inkatha and the elections passed peacefully. I have never seen the hand of God work in such a remarkable way in the political and national level before or since. I am overwhelmed every time I think of those days, and realise that I actually stood in the midst of a Grace Space that God, and a man of God, carved out from the midst of an impending catastrophe.[114]

This was not Grace for an individual or even a small group of people. This was a Grace Space for a nation of over 40 million people. What the nation would eventually do with this Grace Space is another story for another time.

The lesson here is that when God has given a task, never let go. Chase down the goal with every fibre of your being. If, as you are reading these words you are in a dispute of some kind, never give up. Get someone to pray. Don't walk away. God is always working to create the space, amongst the clamouring and arguing voices of mankind, wherein he can demonstrate the marvels of his wondrous Grace.

---

[114] This account is from personal recollections and personal diaries. The dates and statistics are taken from 'A Witness Forever,' a book by Michael Cassidy published by Hodder and Stoughton

Amazing Grace

John Newton [115]

John Newton, once an infidel and libertine, a servant of slaves in Africa, was, by the rich mercy of our Lord and Saviour Jesus Christ, preserved, restored, pardoned, and appointed to preach the faith he had long laboured to destroy!

These are the words that are engraved on the tomb of John Newton in the churchyard of St Paul and St Peter parish church in Olney, Buckinghamshire. This moving epitaph summarizes another remarkable story that reveals the wonderful Grace of God.

John Newton was born on the 24th July 1725 in Wapping London. (Julian Calendar) John's mother was a devoted believer and a loving mother. She taught John to read and write in English and Latin. She made sure he accompanied her to the nearby Independent Chapel. Her sincere prayer was that her son would grow up to be a preacher of the Gospel. It would eventually happen but a shameful and lengthy odyssey lay beforehand.

His mother died when he was 7 years old. His father quickly remarried but the love and spiritual guidance he had known was gone forever. Aged 11 he went to sea as a cabin boy in his father's ship. And so began his swift decline into the coarse and Godless ways of an 18th century seaman.

---

[115] The information in this section is as a result of the authors visit to the Cowper and Newton Museum in Olney, Buckinghamshire and the nearby Church of St Peter and St Paul where Newton laboured from 1764-1780. Dates and finer details are from the book 'Through Many Dangers' by B H Edwards

After sometime on merchantmen he was 'impressed' [116] into the navy. Life on board an 18th century warship was appalling, the men were underfed, over-worked and mercilessly disciplined. Newton gave as good as he got and even when he gained promotion he ruled with the same ruthlessness as he had received. All thoughts of God and a godly life had slowly drained from his mind, he did what he had to do, and dedicated himself to whatever pleasure came his way.

After some time, Newton managed to get exchanged [117] on board a merchantman called the *Pegasus.* What Newton did not know, but soon discovered, was that he was now on board a vessel involved in the slave-trade.

The slave trade worked by taking a cargo of domestic utensils, clothes, and weapons from England to the west Coast of Africa. These were the coastlands of what would become, Liberia, Nigeria, Cameroun, Ghana and Angola. There the goods would be exchanged with agents for enslaved men and women, who would then be taken over to the West Indies to work on the plantations. The human cargo were already slaves before they boarded the ships. They were captives from tribal wars. Those that controlled them saw the trade as a lucrative business, as they gained commodities from England and unloaded troublesome captives. From the West Indies the ships would then take on the sugar and tobacco and other produce and return to England. Then the journey was repeated. The entire journey could take a year or more.

Eventually captaining his own ship, Newton was to be engaged in the slave trade for about 9 years. The details of

---

[116] That was the practice of abducting men and forcing them to serve on warships.

[117] This was a practice, at sea whereby captains could exchange crew members in order to gain certain skills or to unload rebellious seaman for someone else to worry about.

the debauchery in which Newton was now involved, in his own words, '*Are best buried in eternal silence.*' For about a period of 1 year he fell foul of other slave traders and was actually enslaved himself. He was miraculously relieved of his misfortune by the arrival of a ship called the *Greyhound,* commanded by a friend of his father.

Throughout the period of his involvement in the slave trade God was intent on fulfilling the prayers of his late mother. Like Saul of Tarsus, God had placed goads along the way to prod the prodigal into a different direction and eventually arrest him with loving grace. One of these goads was coming across a book entitled 'The Imitation of Christ' by Thomas a Kempis. It brought back thoughts of his Christian childhood and troubled his hardened conscience for a while.

He had a sweetheart at home, Mary Catletts. They had an understanding, but by now he had all but given up any hope of seeing her again, and if he did see her, he thought she would have probably have gone with someone else, and anyway why should such a decent and godly woman look at him now, a person as vile as he.

And then came the experience that finally penetrated the heart of stone. So impacting was this experience that the date is recorded. 10th March 1748. [118]

The Greyhound was caught in a violent storm in the mid-Atlantic. A gigantic wave smashed one side of the ship and filled it with water. The pounding waves smashed against damaged timbers; thread-bare sails were shredded in merciless winds. The ship wallowed in the sea its deck barely above the water. Newton was lashed to the helm for hours to stop him being swept overboard, desperately trying to steer the ship on a reasonable course. He had to try and steer the

---

[118] Julian Calendar. The present calendar was not adopted until 1752

ship and keep the damaged side away from the force of the gale. It was there in the middle of the Atlantic in the violence of the storm, lashed to the helm, that Newton heard the voice of God for the first time in years. He began to recall all the encounters he had with God's Grace and how he had despised and rejected them all. As people do in such state of mind, he began to question if he had gone too far and there was no redemption for him. For four more weeks the battered ship remained afloat, just. Supplies were pitiful, everyday could well have been their last.

In the few moments of respite Newton had from the near hopeless task of keeping the ship afloat, he turned to the Bible and other spiritual books that happened to be on board. God spoke to him and he gained the assurance of salvation. Miraculously the *Greyhound* made landfall near to Londonderry. Newton urgently made his way to a church and through confession and repentance he found the peace with God his soul so craved. He vowed from that day forward he would only serve God.

God had carved out a Grace Space, on the one side was the storm and the fear of imminent drowning, and on the other was the guilt and shame of his prolificacy, the Grace he had spurned and the eternal condemnation that awaited him, and in the middle a place where he encountered the amazing Grace of God. This was the first Grace Space that God created for John since childhood. It wasn't the last, other interventions would be necessary.

After such an encounter we could expect the story of John Newton to embrace divine service. But it was not so. In a few months he was back in his old ways and once again in the slave trade. As captain of his ship, he had much time to contemplate things. He read extensively and studied hard to become fluent in Latin. Each Sunday he held a service on deck with the crew. It was in the quietness of the long nights at sea that God created a second Grace Space for John Newton.

He wrestled with the idea of being a captain of a slave ship and all that it entailed, and being a true Christian. His ship was probably the most 'humane' slave ship afloat, but there was no pretending he was doing anything else except trading in human flesh. Despite his strengthening faith and his vastly improved morality it seems he could not tear himself away from the slave trade. It was, at the time an accepted business, and paid well. God had to dramatically intervene again.

At the age of 30, just before another voyage, he was stricken with a seizure, stroke, or heart attack, exactly what is unknown, but it was enough to render him incapable of returning to sea. He had never had such an episode before or afterwards and so it was seen as a Divine Intervention.

This was the third and final Grace Space necessary to complete his journey to a lasting faith and transformation of life. He attended the preaching of the great evangelicals of his day and sought their counsel and instruction. This included George Whitfield. As he developed his faith he worked as a customs official in Liverpool. Eventually he was ordained in to the ministry of the Church of England and was firstly appointed to Olney in Buckinghamshire and finally to Woolnoth in London. It was here that he threw his significant weight behind the Clapham Sect and William Wilberforce in order to achieve the passing of the bill for the Abolition of Slavery.

The grace of God that John Newton experienced can be best conveyed through his hymns which were often reflections on his journey of faith. Most famous of all, of course is the ever popular, 'Amazing Grace,' the lines of which speak volumes about Newtons experiences with God.

Amazing grace! how sweet the sound,

that saved a wretch like me!
I once was lost, but now am found,
was blind, but now I see.

'Twas grace that taught my heart to fear,
and grace my fears relieved;
How precious did that grace appear
the hour I first believed!

Thro' many dangers, toils, and snares,
I have already come;
'Tis grace hath brought me safe thus far,
and grace will lead me home.

The Lord has promised good to me,
His word my hope secures;
He will my shield and portion be
as long as life endures.

Yes, when this flesh and heart shall fail,
and mortal life shall cease;
I shall possess, within the veil,
a life of joy and peace.

The earth shall soon dissolve like snow,
the sun forbear to shine;
But God, who called me here below,
will be forever mine.[119]

Unfortunately, the second hymn I have chosen, '*In Evil Long I took Delight*' has not retained the popularity of 'Amazing Grace' but I would suggest it is even more explicit of his conversion experience.

In evil long I took delight, unawed by shame or fear,
Till a new object struck my sight, and stopped my wild career.

---

[119] Olney Hymns

I saw One hanging on a tree, in agony and blood,
Who fixed His languid eyes on me, as near His cross I stood.

Sure, never to my latest breath, can I forget that look;
It seemed to charge me with His death, though not a word He
spoke.

My conscience felt and owned the guilt, and plunged me in
despair,
I saw my sins His blood had spilt, and helped to nail Him there.

A second look He gave, which said, I freely all forgive;
This blood is for thy ransom paid; I die that thou mayst live.

Thus, while His death my sin displays in all its blackest hue,
Such is the mystery of grace, it seals my pardon too.

With pleasing grief and mournful joy, my spirit now is filled,
That I should such a life destroy, yet live by Him I killed.[120]

In the story of John Newton, we learn about the *persistence* of God's Grace. Although Newton recounts the experience in the storm on the *Greyhound* as the pivotal moment in his conversion, God came to him dramatically on several occasions, and indeed it was necessary for God to do so. We can learn from this that if Grace is once despised it does not mean that it is no longer available. It may mean the road to the next Grace Space is more traumatic, but there will be another Grace Space. As God reached down into the eye of an Atlantic storm, the stillness of the captain's cabin, and the shock of a medical emergency, so he can meet with us in the many dangers toils and snares we have to face.

It may be asked, 'Why Newton?' Why not another seaman or even the slaves themselves? I don't know. But what I do know is, his mothers' prayers which were stilled on earth some 25

---

[120] Olney Hymns

years previously, were not forgotten by God. They still echoed around the heavenly courts. Never stop praying and pleading for the soul of a loved one.

I will close this section with two more quotes from Newton himself;

I am not what I ought to be. Ah! how imperfect and deficient. I am not what I might be, considering my privileges and opportunities.
I am not what I wish to be. God, who knows my heart; knows I wish to be like Him. I am not what I hope to be. Before long, I will drop this clay tabernacle, to be like Him and see Him as He is! Yet, I am not what I once was; a child of sin, and slave of the devil! Though not all these; not what I ought to be, not what I might be, not what I wish or hope to be, and not what I once was. I think I can truly say with the apostle, By the grace of God I am what I am.

My memory is nearly gone, but I remember two things: that I am a great sinner and that Christ is a great Saviour!

Immaculate Grace

Maximilian Koble. [121]

This story takes us deep into the demonic darkness of the second world war. We have seen that at Nuremburg the accounts were retold. Here is where they actually happened. Come with me to the epicentre of it all, the Auschwitz death camp at the Polish town of Oswiecim, near Krakow. It is situated on a natural island formed by the course of the rivers Sola and Vistula. Today it is a pleasant enough place to be, but in the early 1940's it was the epicentre of spiritual and moral darkness.

---

[121] This account is compiled as result of visiting the Auschwitz death camp and research on the internet.

Raymond Kolbe was born on the 7th of January 1894 in Zadunsks Wola, Poland. Despite the fact that he was physically frail throughout his life, he was a brilliant mathematician and physicist. In 1915 he received a Doctorate in Philosophy when aged 21. In 1907 he entered a Franciscan order as a novitiate and took the name Maximillian. He was ordained as a Priest in 1918 and awarded a doctorate in Theology in 1919.

He was an extremely conservative minded priest. He was devoted to the veneration of the Immaculate Virgin Mary. It was, in being faced with the story of Maximillian Kolbe, that I learned to make my protestant heckles lie down at the mention of venerating Mary. I don't understand the process of such a belief, but I learned that my finite mind will never understand everything. I cannot criticise Maximillian Kolbe unless I have done what he did. The fact is, that whatever Kolbe believed in regard to the Virgin Mary, it led him to demonstrate one of the most exceptional acts of Christlikeness the world has ever seen.

He was radically anti-communist. He founded various religious orders and monasteries and publish many papers. During the early 1930's he continued his ministry in Japan. In 1936 he returned to Poland. He had become an influential writer and broadcaster and as can be expected he opposed the rising power of Naziism.

When Poland fell in 1939 Kolbe and his friars became the target of the occupiers. He refused to submit to Nazi sanctions and was arrested on the 17th February 1941 in Warsaw. On May 28th 1941 he was transferred to the notorious death camp at Auschwitz. Here his name was changed once again. He was no longer Raymond or Maximillian but simple 16670, a number tattooed on his arm.

A few years ago, I stood at the doorway of a semi subterranean room in one of the ghastly prison blocks at Auschwitz. Two large candles burned inside. The guide simply said, '*This is where Maximillian Kolbe died,*' in such a way as if everyone should have known who Maximillian Kolbe was. Maybe they did, but at the time I did not. I sensed something had happened here I needed to know more about. My ignorance made me promise myself to find out.

Despite being now infected with T.B. and Typhus, Kolbe was put to hard labour. Starved and diseased he continued to minister to the tragic souls around him according to the beliefs he held. He was known as the most loved man in Auschwitz by Catholics, Protestants, Jews, Poles, Russians, and Gypsies alike.

On July 31st 1941 a prisoner from Kolbe's block managed to escape. As punishment SS-Hauptsturmführer Karl Fritzsch ordered that 10 men were to be chosen at random to be starved to death. The prisoners stood in rows at the notorious parade area in the middle of those haunting wooden huts, clothed in those filthy, hideous, striped pyjama-like uniforms with which we have become familiar from films. One of the men selected for starvation was Franciszek Gajowniczek, a 39-year-old Polish army sergeant. Gajowniczek broke down and pleaded with the officers to let him go. He had a wife and child at home. In the confusion Maximillian Kolbe stepped forward from the ranks and approached the officer and said, '*Let him go, I will die in his place.*' Flustered at the unprecedented turn of events, the officer agreed, and so Kolbe was taken to his death with the others.

In the darkest of times Kolbe took the weight of the Nazi atrocities on his frail shoulder, along with all the bitterness, hatred, and demonic antipathy and pushed it aside and created a Grace Space. So, he demonstrated the words of

Jesus when he said, '*Greater love has no man than this, than a man lay down his life for his friends.*' John 15:13.

This is why I have called it 'Immaculate Grace' because there is no demonstration of Grace that is greater than the surrender of one's own life for the benefit of others. I have seen an actor acting out this scene, and that is moving enough, but to have been there that day would have been to stand both in hell and heaven, and to touch the hands of angels and demons, at the same time.

Kolbe was taken to the death-cell. After two weeks with no food or water all the other men had died. Kolbe prayed and ministered to them all. Kolbe was injected with carbolic acid and died on the 14th of August 1941 aged 47 years. He was dispatched to the ovens the following day.

Gajowniczek lived until 1995. He witnessed the beatification of Maximillian Kolbe in 1971 and his Canonisation in 1982. When interviewed at the ceremony of Canonisation Gajowniczek simply said, '*He died for me!*'

I have often asked, Could I have done that? 'Would I have done that?' John 13:37-38. Peter said he would. Jesus said to him, 'will you really.' Well yes, he did.

That act was, in my opinion, louder, longer and more convicting, than all the sermons ever preached. Amid the stench and horror of that infernal place a Grace Space was created, and the Grace of God inspired a Catholic Priest to paint a beautiful picture that should be engraved on the heart of every believer. Calvary was demonstrated at Auschwitz. Not by a prisoner painting on a cell wall, or by a Priest administering communion, but by a man actually laying down his life in the most horrific way, so that another may live.

Grace what have You done, murdered for me on that cross
Accused in absence of wrong my sin washed away in Your blood
Too much to make sense of it all
I know that Your love breaks my fall
The scandal of grace You died in my place, so my soul will live [122]

Generous Grace

Pastor Uwe Holmer. [123]

My own lifetime has spanned sufficient years to enable me to remember, as a child, the fear and trepidation those around me felt when the Berlin Wall was erected in 1961, and the exhilaration of its downfall in 1989.

I remember well, being at a summer convention in 1961. There were a group of people present from what had just become East Germany. As they departed to go home to an uncertain future, the wave of emotion that emanated from the crowd of people as they prayed for them, has never left me. I was a child but I could sense that something was very foreboding.

What went on behind the wall in the intervening years has been the subject of many films and books, some in the form of documentaries, others dramatized accounts. Once again let me emphasise this is neither a history or biography. It is a story of Grace. It is not the only story of Grace from this arena, but is the one that has impacted me. It is a story of a Grace Space like no other.

Erich Honecker was the leader of the DDR, [124] better known

---

[122] Hillsong. Joel Houston and Matt Crocker
[123] The Upward Look John Forrest. The Fall; the end of Honecker. Eric Friedler. Candles behind the wall. B. Elliot.
[124] Deutsche Demokratische Republik, East Germany.

as East Germany, from 1976 until his overthrow in 1989. However, he had been involved in the politics of the Communist Sector of Germany since the end of the second world war. To his credit he forged a state that was arguably more prosperous than any other Soviet satellite state, but that is a scant compliment. However, he was ruthless. He was the force behind the construction of the infamous Berlin Wall in 1961. He had no qualms about torturing and massacring his own citizens if they stepped out of line. The state was particularly repressive of Christian believers. His wife Margot was minister of Education.

Uwe Holmer was born in 1929 in what was to become East Germany. He was a Lutheran Pastor. Holmer suffered along with other evangelicals from the restrictions of the DDR. His children were denied further education because they were Christians.

In 1989 the Soviet Union fell. The Berlin Wall was dismantled and Germany was re-united. Honecker and his wife were the most hated people in Germany from both sides of the divide. Several lawsuits were laid against him but for various reasons were not pursued. He was terminally ill with cancer. Eventually he was expelled from office and found himself on the streets, homeless. No one would take them in. He applied to a Lutheran Charity for accommodation. It was thought inappropriate as they feared public unrest. It was then that Pastor Uwe Holmer came forward and offered the former dictator accommodation in his own home. Honecker and his wife stayed in the Holmer's home from 30th January to the 3rd of April 1990.

There was public outrage. The house was often surrounded by angry mobs. Holmer was threatened and vilified, but he stood firm, believing he was doing what Jesus would have done. People did not understand this act of Grace on someone so undeserving. To quote Holmer:

The Lord has charged us to follow him and take in all those who are troubled and burdened and to follow his commandment and love our enemies, and to live by the prayer he taught us, forgive us our trespasses as we forgive those who trespass against us. We want to live by Christ's example.

By faith, Holmer created a Grace Space. The years of atrocities and personal pain were pushed to one side and the outrage of the population to the other and he created a space where he could show the love of Christ. What was unique on this occasion was that the love of Christ made no difference to the hardened dictator and his wife. I suppose they were grateful for the hospitality, but they didn't find God in it. Honecker eventually found asylum in Chile which is where he died in 1994.

Of course, Honecker and his wife did not deserve it. If they had deserved it, it would not have been Grace. Grace can only be displayed on the undeserving as pardon can only be bestowed on the guilty. This display of Grace was done simply because Jesus commanded it to be done. There was no guarantee of it achieving anything, and in the end, what was achieved was difficult for many to understand.

This story teaches us that it is our responsibility as believers to create Grace Spaces where undeserving people can have the opportunity to experience God's Grace. It is not our responsibility to only show grace to those who are likely to respond positively towards it. It takes us into the heart of the Lord Jesus, who suffered upon Calvary's Cross without any assurance that anyone would ever believe on him. Of all the people he had ministered God's grace to, only a handful were found at the crucifixion. John 19:25. There would be no more on the day of the resurrection. Should he have not taken the 'angel option' and forgotten the whole idea? Matthew 26:53.

Serving as a hospital Chaplain for several years I learned to let God help me to create a Grace Space for everyone, whatever their belief, lifestyle, or state of mind. It was not my responsibility what they did with the Grace Space, but it was my responsibility to create one. Why? Because a Grace Space is the only place on earth where people can possibly catch a glimpse of Jesus. Yes, some of those did not deserve Grace. It was their fault they were where they were. But I hope we have learned through these stories that being 'undeserving' is the precise qualification required to receive Grace.

May this account bring us to the place where we can abandon feelings of self-righteousness and judgment of others. No one deserves God's Grace, not even ourselves, we make a Grace Spaces because Jesus told us to, and the rest is His business. Far too often we assume the role of the unforgiving servant. Matthew 18:21-35, or the self-righteous elder brother in Luke 15. We can be quite happy to receive forgiveness from God for our sins, but unwilling to forgive those who have sinned against us. We judge that our sins are lesser than those committed against us, so we deserve Grace, those who offend us only deserve justice. Many need repentance from this state of mind.

> *Marvellous, infinite, matchless grace,*
> *Freely bestowed on all who believe!*
> *You that are longing to see His face,*
> *Will you this moment His grace receive?*
> *Grace, grace, God's grace,*
> *Grace that will pardon and cleanse within;*
> *Grace, grace, God's grace,*
> *Grace that is greater than all our sin!* [125]

---

[125] Juliet Johnson. Grace Greater than our sin.

The Grace Space

CHAPTER THIRTEEN.

The Grace in which we stand.

After this lengthy odyssey, I will offer a statement describing the Richness of His Grace.

God saw before him all the events of time. He saw that he could create a people who would live in such a way as to resemble his character and bring endless Glory to His Name. He saw that these people would however fall from righteousness to sin, this would become universal, and so mankind would become incapable of pleasing, serving or even approaching him.

God saw that if he gave a gift powerful enough to overcome man's inability to believe, an atonement, myriads of people would seek to renew fellowship with him. He decided to grant a gift of faith which could enable the sons and daughters of Adam to believe.

God created a Grace Space by appointing a Saviour to bear the sins of the whole world by becoming the atoning sacrifice for everyone. By exercising the gift of faith that enabled belief, anyone could step into this relationship that God alone had provided out of the love of his own heart for mankind whom he had made. He forced apart the depravity of mankind and the righteous sentences that were their just reward, and made a space wherein mankind could be exposed to Divine Grace and receive the faith to believe and be saved.

As he saw faith working in these people, who would respond by their own autonomous free-will, he designed a destiny for them and promised to himself that nothing, neither things in heaven, on earth, or in hell, would stop him fulfilling this destiny for them. He chose these people to be able to enjoy a special and privileged relationship with himself that would amaze the universe.

God proclaimed his message of grace through patriarchs, prophets, kings and priests, the Messiah, his own Son, Jesus, and a group of men he named apostles and their successors. Whoever heard this message and allowed the gift of faith God had placed within them to operate would be cleansed from their sin and adopted into his extended family as sons of God.

God also saw that there would be many who would not receive the message of Grace, and refuse to believe. He reserved the right to bring upon them a righteous judgment, which at the end of days would banish them forever from his presence.

To me the words of the great hymn written by Judson W. Van DeVenter describe the act of conversion most succinctly:

All to Jesus I surrender, All to Him I freely give;
I will ever love and trust Him, In His presence daily live.

I surrender all, I surrender all;
All to Thee, my blessed Saviour,
I surrender all.

All to Jesus I surrender, Humbly at His feet I bow;
Worldly pleasures all forsaken, take me, Jesus, take me now.

All to Jesus I surrender, make me, Saviour, wholly Thine;
Let me feel the Holy Spirit, truly know that Thou art mine.

All to Jesus I surrender, Lord, I give myself to Thee;
Fill me with Thy love and power, Let Thy blessing fall on me.

All to Jesus I surrender, Now I feel the sacred flame;
Oh, the joy of full salvation! Glory, glory, to His Name! [126]

The Grace in which we stand.

This is the ground that all the Fathers of the faith we have mentioned desired to stand upon. From the liberality of Pelagius to the strictures of Calvin, they all sought to describe and experience the Ground of Grace. To all, it was the goal which they longed for.

Therefore, having been justified by faith, we have peace with God through our Lord Jesus Christ, through whom also we have access by faith into this grace in which we stand, and rejoice in hope of the glory of God. And not only that, but we also glory in tribulations, knowing that tribulation produces perseverance; and perseverance, character; and character, hope. Now hope does not disappoint, because the love of God has been poured out in our hearts by the Holy Spirit who was given to us.
Romans 5:1-5.

---

[126] J v.d.Venter. Redemption Hymnal 600

And the same verse, beautifully rendered in another version.

> *Our faith in Jesus transfers God's righteousness to us and he now declares us flawless in his eyes. This means we can now enjoy true and lasting peace with God, all because of what our Lord Jesus, the Anointed One, has done for us. Our faith guarantees us permanent access into this marvellous kindness that has given us a perfect relationship with God. What incredible joy bursts forth within us as we keep on celebrating our hope of experiencing God's glory!*
> *But that's not all! Even in times of trouble we have a joyful confidence, knowing that our pressures will develop in us patient endurance. And patient endurance will refine our character, and proven character leads us back to hope.*
> Romans 5:1-5. The Passion Translation.

The first experience of Grace is Peace with God.

There are few things more spiritually therapeutic than having prayed a prayer of confession and repentance to rise and sense the fact that the guilt has been cancelled and we are at peace with God. It is like the removal of a blockage, or the lifting of a heavy burden. Such an experience of course, is only possible when we pray in faith believing that God is listening and dealing with us according to his word. Salvation goes beyond the fact that sins are forgiven and that eternal life is guaranteed. Salvation forges a relationship between the believer and God.

There is an incompatibility between God and man. It is similar if two people meet, one with left wing views and one with right wing views. Or an anti-abortionist and a pro-abortionist. Or whatever incompatibility of thought you wish. The only way a peaceful conversation can be held is if they do not talk about the issues that divide them. The fundamental issue between God and man is sin, and unless that is addressed there is no peace. Many people believe they get on well with God, but they never deal with the main issue. We are declared to be free from the guilt of sin when we by faith believe that Jesus died for us. The just for the unjust, the sinless for the sinful, the righteous for the unrighteous. That his sufferings and death are the equivalent to the suffering and death of every person that ever lived, for their sins. Whether we are following Augustine, Luther, Calvin, or Arminius; whether we are Catholic, Protestant, or Orthodox, it makes no difference, unless there has been a Divine exchange of our sin for Christ's righteousness we are not at peace with God.

We are at peace because we are now travelling in the same direction; we agree on what really matters; we have the same aims and objectives; and we have the same view of the world around us.

The second experience is access by Faith into Grace.

The scriptures speak of people who feel they *have done enough.* "We are Abraham's children," the Pharisees protested. John 8:33. In fact Jesus replied, "You are the children of the enemy of God." (the Devil) John 8: 44. They were convinced enough had been done. They were born into the faith. They were observant of the rules of the faith. But they had no relationship with God.

There was a time in Christian history when that would have been enough to identify them among the Elect. They knew the religion but they didn't know the Father. Salvation requires a spiritual encounter. The crux of that encounter is that you recognise who Jesus is. Jesus reasoned that if the people accepted him; they would also accept the Father. If they rejected him; they also rejected the Father. John 6:40. By rejecting Jesus they were rejecting what we have called 'enabling faith.' They were children of the enemy, because they rejected Jesus.

The scriptures speak of a people who feel they *have not done enough.* To contrast with the above, there is the story of the man who came to Jesus and said he had done all that the men in the previous group had done yet he knew deep down it was not enough. Mark 10: 17-22. This man was in a better position because he realised there was something missing. The answer could be said in this way; "You have to learn to trust God's words for your salvation and not your deeds." He was nearer, but not there yet. He had received 'enabling faith' but he was still on the journey.

The scriptures speak of people who feel they *can never do enough.* Jesus told a parable of two men going to pray. Luke 18: 9-14. The first was much like the two we have mentioned. The second however was different.

> *And the tax collector, standing afar off, would not so much as raise his eyes to heaven, but beat his breast, saying, 'God, be merciful to me a sinner!' I tell you, this man went down to his house justified rather than the other; for everyone who exalts himself will be humbled, and he who humbles himself will be exalted."* Luke 18: 13-14.

This man was justified. That is, he found peace with God. How? By acknowledging the fundamental problem, he was a sinner. Bowing his head in shame and guilt for his sin. Understanding there was nothing he could do except asking God for Mercy. (*a grace word*) This man went to his house exalted, lifted up, elevated in spirit. He had received enabling faith and had touched the heart of God.

Perform whatever symbolic ritual you wish, as long as it is a genuine symbol of the Gospel message, and as long as you do it with faith and gratitude in your heart for what Jesus has done. *Whatsoever is not of Faith is sin.* Romans 14:23.

I have been baptised, I partake of the Eucharist, I have confessed sin to a brother, I have received ash on my head at Lent. I have been anointed and also anoint with oil. I have baptised both infants and adults. I have administered Extreme Unction. I have made the sign of the cross over the living and the dead, and myself, with the fingers correctly positioned. But if I did any of these things without the faith in that I am saved through what Jesus did, and that anything that was transmitted to others was not through what I did, but what Jesus did for them. Then it is no more than idolatry, and therefore sin.

We can stand in Grace. Not cower in a corner in case we are noticed, or hold on to it by our fingertips. We can stand firm in the centre of God's Grace because we are triumphs of his Grace, cleansed through his blood and filled with his Spirit. We are trophies of his Grace, brands from the burning, rescued from the mire and the clay, re-created in the likeness of the Son of God. In the face of all earth, heaven and hell, God says, this is what my Grace can do!

The third is the hope of the Glory of God.

To stand in Grace through Faith enables us to catch a glimpse of our destiny. We know that the believer is predestined. That is, our destiny is guaranteed. It is an extension of the Grace in which we stand. Grace stretches out into eternity and is as safe and secure there as it is right now. The hope of the glory of God was manifested when Jesus rose from the dead. The risen Jesus was the guarantee of eternal life and the final triumph of believers over sin and death.

> *A little while longer and the world will see Me no more, but you will see Me. Because I live, you will live also.* John 14:19.

Glory, is the splendour, acclaim, illustriousness and honour of the risen Jesus. He stepped into a dimension of life where the hands of wicked men could no longer touch him, the chains of death could not hold him and the demons of hell must bow before him. The pathway he has walked has blazed a trail for us to follow. He is our fore-runner. As sure as he has gone ahead, we will follow.

> *There is one glory of the sun, another glory of the moon, and another glory of the stars; for one star differs from another star in glory. So also is the resurrection of the dead. The body is sown in corruption, it is raised in incorruption; it is sown in dishonour; it is raised in glory. It is sown in weakness; it is raised in power. It is sown a natural body; it is raised a spiritual body. There is a natural body, and there is a spiritual body. And so, it is written, "The first man Adam became a living being." The last Adam became a life-giving spirit.*
> *However, the spiritual is not first, but the natural, and afterward the spiritual. The first man was of the earth, made of dust; the second Man is the Lord from heaven. As was the man of dust, so also are those who are made of dust; and as is the heavenly Man, so also are those who are heavenly. And as we have borne the image of the man of dust, we shall also bear the image of the heavenly Man.* 1 Corinthians 15:41-49.

The fourth is the desire to persevere.

The Grace Space is sufficient to cancel the guilt of our sin and keep us through whatever trials and temptations we may have to endure until we see Jesus face to face. But we have to stay in the Grace Space. An astronaut can go to the moon and walk around freely as long as he wears his protective suit. Inside it he has a safe atmosphere that will keep him alive. If he takes it off, he will die. As our salvation was foreknown by God when he saw us 'in Christ' that is, in relationship with him, our perseverance is also 'in Christ.'

Eternal Security.

The dominant view that emerged from the Reformation described such a relationship between the believer and the saviour as being Eternally Secure. The bond that had been formed through divine election and manifest in time by the persons conversion, could never be revoked. It was believed that anyone who fell away from the faith were never really saved in the first place. This is a logical conclusion of the position that placed the origin of salvation in the act of predestination. Any scripture verses that spoke of falling away, spoke of this scenario.

It amounted to the fact that although believers should manifest the fruits of the Holy Spirit, if they did not, they would not lose their salvation. What would happen, however, was that in the judgements of believers, they would be deprived of the blessings of the faithful and meted out some disciplinary sentence in order that they may become holy. A sort of purgatory none the less!

It is argued, as the work of salvation was entirely a work of God without human participation, so the preserving or persevering of the saints was also entirely a work of God. There are many scriptures that describe a such relationship with God that is eternally secure and irrevocable. Here are examples of them.

> *What then shall we say to these things? If God is for us, who can be against us? He who did not spare His own Son, but delivered Him up for us all, how shall He not with Him also freely give us all things? Who shall bring a charge against God's elect? It is God who justifies. Who is he who condemns? It is Christ who died, and furthermore is also risen, who is even at the right hand of God, who also makes intercession for us. Who shall separate us from the love of Christ? Shall tribulation, or distress, or persecution, or famine, or nakedness, or peril, or sword? As it is written: "For Your sake we are killed all day long; we are accounted as sheep for the slaughter."*
> *Yet in all these things we are more than conquerors through Him who loved us. For I am persuaded that neither death nor life, nor angels nor principalities nor powers, nor things present nor things to come, nor height nor depth, nor any other created*

thing, shall be able to separate us from the love of God which is in Christ Jesus our Lord. Romans 8:31-39.

In Him you also trusted, after you heard the word of truth, the gospel of your salvation; in whom also, having believed, you were sealed with the Holy Spirit of promise, who is the guarantee of our inheritance until the redemption of the purchased possession, to the praise of His glory. Ephesians 1:13-14.

My sheep hear My voice, and I know them, and they follow Me. And I give them eternal life, and they shall never perish; neither shall anyone snatch them out of My hand. My Father, who has given them to Me, is greater than all; and no one is able to snatch them out of My Father's hand. I and My Father are one. John 10:27-30.

Conditional Security.

But then again there are verses that state the opposite and propose something we can call Conditional Security. Here it is agreed that the act of salvation and the subsequent works of Grace are all a work of God, a human response is necessary for it to be maintained.

> *Therefore, leaving the discussion of the elementary principles of Christ, let us go on to perfection, not laying again the foundation of repentance from dead works and of faith toward God, of the doctrine of baptisms, of laying on of hands, of resurrection of the dead, and of eternal judgment. And this we will do if God permits.*
>
> *For it is impossible for those who were once enlightened, and have tasted the heavenly gift, and have become partakers of the Holy Spirit, and have tasted the good word of God and the powers of the age to come, if they fall away, to renew them again to repentance, since they crucify again for themselves the Son of God, and put Him to an open shame.* Hebrews 6: 1-6.
>
> *For if, after they have escaped the pollutions of the world*

through the knowledge of the Lord and Saviour Jesus Christ, they are again entangled in them and overcome, the latter end is worse for them than the beginning. For it would have been better for them not to have known the way of righteousness, than having known it, to turn from the holy commandment delivered to them. 2 Peter 2: 20-21.

The problem arises as we have already mentioned is in where we consider the salvation of the individual originates. To say it originates in the will of God to choose a certain number to be saved, then it is logical that once those people are saved it cannot be undone. They are preserved by the persevering acts of God's Grace to keep them in all circumstances.

However, if the salvation originates in the free decision of the individual to co-operate with the gift of faith, then it is equally logical to accept that there is the possibility that decision can be revoked. Here the perseverance is in the devotion and discipline of the believer to honour God in all they do.

The weakness of the former is twofold. It may lead to a view that once saved, one can live how one wishes, in the end there will be a process that will bring them to salvation. It may also lead to a legalistic approach to observance of traditions which are claimed to be manifestations of Grace, but in reality, can require some considerable human effort to achieve.

The weakness of the latter is that it proposes that the human will can turn what is declared as something eternal, to that which is merely temporal. In so doing one can slip in and out of Grace at will and receive no absolute assurance of salvation.

It is important to point out that in the passages that emphasise Eternal Security it clearly says that no force from outside of the believer, from heaven, hell, or earth, is powerful enough to negate the love of God. In the passages that speak of Conditional Security, the forces that would cause such falling are not from outside the believer but from within. Galatians 5:16-21 list things that could cause such a scenario.

Such an understanding is perfectly compatible with what we have expressed on 'Devolved Sovereignty.' Paul's glorious 'staircase' to security in Romans 8:29-39 has as its first step '*those whom he foreknew.*' That is, those whom he knew beforehand would respond positively to Grace through faith, and remain embraced by Grace, and would triumph in Grace. They are eternally secure, but as in all relationships, the human will and the Divine will each have a part to play.

The verses in Hebrews 6:1-6, describe an extreme situation with several stages of apostacy. Sadly, I have known it to happen, but it is not the usual thing. More often there may be one of these things in some measure.

The second point is that there is a place of no return. But as much as we do not know who will accept the Gospel in the first place, we do not know who has reached this point either, so Grace remains extended to all.

The third point is that there is no way back for anyone who has reneged on their profession of faith, to whatever degree, except to go back to the cross and start again.

The fourth point is that for '*those going on to maturity*' there is a security in Grace that endures for time and eternity.

I believe in Eternal Security guaranteed as a result of our ongoing relationship with Jesus Christ. I believe in the possibility of falling beyond the scope of God's Grace, having once embraced it, by severing the relationship with Jesus Christ of my own free will. In such a situation I know I can blame no one else in heaven, earth or hell, it is entirely a yielding of my will to my own depravity.

The proponents of unconditional Eternal security, typically, snap at our heels here and seek to unsettle us with uncertainty. Their *certainty* lies in what has been construed from Calvin, saying that God has secured salvation for some and secured damnation for others. That is a certainty I wish to do without. Rather I embrace the certainty that God has offered Grace to all and that Grace of itself, is sufficient to keep all who come, both now and throughout all eternity. The fact remains that all who hear will not come and all who come will not stay. But neither affect the sufficiency of Grace to save and to preserve those who have believed and continue to believe.

> *Brethren, if anyone among you wanders from the truth, and someone turns him back, let him know that he who turns a sinner from the error of his way will save a soul from death and cover a multitude of sins.* James 5:19-20.

Here, 'the falling away,' is not considered as some lapse that can be corrected in a future experience. The lapse is crucial. It means the person concerned faces eternal death. It can only be corrected by repentance in this life.

> *For the grace of God that brings salvation has appeared to all men, teaching us that, denying ungodliness and worldly lusts, we should live soberly, righteously, and godly in the present age, looking for the blessed hope and glorious appearing of our great God and Saviour Jesus Christ, who gave Himself for us, that He might redeem us from every lawless deed and purify for Himself His own special people, zealous for good works.* Titus 2:11-14.

> *A debtor to mercy alone,*
> *Of covenant mercy I sing,*
> *Nor fear, with God's righteousness on,*
> *My person and offerings to bring.*
> *The terrors of law and of God*

With me can have nothing to do;
My Saviour's obedience and blood
Hide all my transgressions from view.

The work which His goodness began,
The arm of His strength will complete;
His promise is Yea and Amen,
And never was forfeited yet.
Things future, nor things that are now,
Not all things below or above,
Can make Him His purpose forego,
Or sever my soul from His love.

My name from the palms of His hands
Eternity will not erase;
Impressed on His heart, it remains
In marks of indelible grace.
Yes! I to the end shall endure,
As sure as the earnest is given;
More happy, but not more secure,
The glorified spirits in heaven.[127]

We 'Glory in Tribulation.' That is not to say that we welcome and embrace pain in some masochistic way. I am sure Paul did not like to be beaten, imprisoned, and shipwrecked, and neither do we. But Paul could *'take pleasure in his infirmities'* because of the results they procured. What we glory in is the fact that nothing that happens leaves us in an unredeemable state, and everything that happens that humbles the flesh, elevates the spirit.

Paul realised that the opposition he faced was working in his spirit the qualities of virtue, humility, patience, devotion and Christlikeness. As the Lord was *'made perfect through suffering,'* [128] so was he.

---

[127] A M Toplady. Redemption Hymnal 390.
[128] Hebrews 2:10

And we know that all things work together for good to those who love God, to those who are the called according to His purpose. Romans 8:28.

And finally, the in-filling of the Holy Spirit

The Grace Space contains experiences the Bible calls the 'infilling of the Holy Spirit.' Jesus also received the anointing of the Holy Spirit. Isaiah 42:1; Luke 4:14; John 3:34; Acts 10:38; Romans 8:11. Jesus' ministry was done in the power of the Holy Spirit. It was not done in his own strength as the Son of God, because he laid aside that when he became man. Philippians 2:2:7-8. It encourages us when we receive the commission from him to continue his works until he returns, that we can operate under the same anointing. John 20:22; Acts 1:8; 2;33.

The Holy Spirit is called the Spirit of Grace. Zechariah 12:10; Hebrews 10:29. That is, the Holy Spirit demonstrates his presence by giving gifts of Grace, measures of underserved favour. Romans 12:6; 1 Corinthians 1:4.

The Greek word for Grace as we have noted, is *Charis.* The Greek word used in identifying the Gifts of the Holy Spirit is, *Charismata.* One needs to know very little about New Testament Greek in this incidence to see that they come from the same grammatical root. The Gifts of the Holy Spirit are Gifts of Grace. 1 Corinthians 12: 1-11. They are entirely supernatural and cannot be learned or developed. They are to be distinguished from natural gifts of Grace, whereby the inspiration to do things is of the Holy Spirit but the action is human. Romans 12:6-8. They are acts of Grace from one person to another.

Grace as it comes through the work of the Holy Spirit is a many faceted thing.

John 3:8. The Holy Spirit is ultimately a mystery. You can't regulate him; demand he operates through ritual, or know what he will do next. We simply have to be a channel through whom he can move as he desires to move.

John 4: 24. True worship is to be inspired and structured by the Holy Spirit. it doesn't religiously follow as certain procedure. In this context Jesus was saying that it was not the liturgy of Jerusalem or of Mount Gerazim that mattered. It is fresh and relative to the moment, yet faithful to spiritual truth. It is something that arises from Spirit-filled hearts and will not only transform Jews and Samaritans, but people from every nation on earth.

John 14:16. The Spirit as a Helper. Jesus tells us that the Holy Spirit is essentially the same as himself. He is from the same place, the Father; he is about the same business, saving people from sin; and he works in exactly the same way, from the heart. When the Spirit speaks, he says exactly what Jesus would have said. He is 'an undeserved favour' that will be with you and in you until Jesus returns. John 16:13.

Acts 1:8. The coming of the Holy Spirit would be the enduement of power to undertake the task of taking the gospel to the world. The authority of the ministry of the church would not be confined to a hierarchy of church leaders, but bestowed in all who received the Holy Spirit.

Acts 2:3-4. Many say, that this phenomenon of Grace was only for the days in which it happened as a miraculous sign to launch the church among the nations. Actually, it is more likely to be a sign to those who so loudly proclaim God's Sovereignty, that they are in fact afraid of God's Sovereignty, when he inspires them to speak in a language they don't understand. We find the phenomena reoccurs throughout the New Testament, and indeed spasmodically throughout church history to the present day. [129] It is one of the Grace signs that emphasises the supernatural presence of God amongst his people. Acts 10: 44-46; 19:6.

Romans 8:16-17. The Holy Spirit creates that sense of belonging. The assurance that we are truly children of the Living God and heirs to the blessings of his righteous kingdom. This assurance does not come out of the logic of a philosophical argument but as a result of the indwelling presence of the Holy Spirit. It causes me to be sure that he loves me, he has saved me, and he will keep me until I see him face to face.

1 Corinthians 9:19-20. The Grace of the Holy Spirit dispenses of any need for ritual to regulate what we do. We have one desire to glorify God motivated by the One who has taken up residence in the temple of our hearts.

1 Corinthians 12:1-11. The Holy Spirit elevates the words of believers by lifting them to the supernatural realm of words of wisdom, knowledge, prophecy and interpreting unknown languages. The Holy Spirit gives the Grace of healing, and miracles. He gives the Grace of Faith and Discernment of Spirits to equip the believer in his mission.

2 Corinthians 3:17-18. Where the Spirit of the Lord is there is the Grace to transform the believer from one experience of Grace to another. This is the authentic seal of God Grace when lives are changed to be like Jesus.

Ephesians 1:17. The Spirit of wisdom and revelation in the knowledge of him. The Holy Spirit reveals to us more and more of the glory of God through the ongoing outpouring of the Holy Spirit.

---

[129] The Unfailing Stream. Dr. David Allen.

2 Timothy 1:7. A Spirit of power, love and a sound mind. Not of the fear of failure, or the impossibility of the task, but a deep assurance that God will equip those whom he has called to do the task he has laid before them.

This is the 'infilling' of the Holy Spirit. This is what Augustine tried to lay to rest 1600 years ago. This is why he and his interpreters needed such a water-tight philosophical system in which to place their confidence. They side-stepped the Holy Spirit and lost the ongoing dynamism of the gospel.

The Grace Space

CHAPTER FOURTEEN

Becoming People of Grace.

We have spent almost all of this book so far speaking of God's Grace to man. I would like to conclude with some thoughts on the subject of Grace to and from one to the other. In the parable of the unforgiving servant, (Matthew 18: 21-35) Jesus emphasised that we should forgive others because God has forgiven us. In the same way we should act to others as God has acted towards us. As he has shown us Grace, we should show Grace to others.

We have noted how the belief in a limited atonement and irresistible Grace produced a limited gospel. Although the gospel was preached to whoever would hear, there remained a disposition towards slavery, sectarianism, chauvinism, and racism for many years. Our emphasis on a universal atonement and resistible Grace, lead us to the understanding that there can be no limit and no exclusions to the Grace we are called upon to show to our fellow human beings.

Grace without God.

Something that has developed out of 19th century philanthropy are the large organised Charities. They were mostly birthed from the compassion of people of faith. Some still hold to their Christian values, others have evolved to become more secular. Most Churches in the UK are Charities, but there are many Charities which have no official Christian link. We are seeing something that appears to me to be, *'Grace without God.'* Let me say very clearly that any organisation that reaches out to the neglected, abused, or under-privileged needs all the support they can get, whatever their spiritual commitment or religious belief that motivates them.

As I write this book there is an advert on the media in the UK asking for support for a well-deserving charity, that begins with a person saying, *'You know that warm feeling you get when you help someone in need?'* Once again, I do not wish to criticise in any way what these people are doing, their work is admirable. Simply to point out that Grace is described here as motivated by the feeling it gives the giver, not by the example of Jesus Christ.

In our sharing of Grace, we must be careful that the objective of showing the love of Christ for those in need is not clouded over. Our acts of Grace are not acts of saving Grace in themselves, but hopefully they are demonstrations of what saving Grace would be like if the person believed. As we show Christlikeness, let us pray that Christlikeness will be seen for what it is, and not just people being nice to one another.

Grace in Speech

Let your speech always be with grace, seasoned with salt Colossians 4:6

That is, speech that presents undeserved favour. Our speech is so important. We can give an impression of ourselves before anyone comes near us, because sound travels. I have heard people say things that caused me to determine that I had no need to get any closer to them. How incredible when we heard words that said, 'I need to get to know that person.' Words of Grace are kind, uplifting, encouraging, affirming, dignified, healing, and embracing. Even if words need to be in the form of correction or rebuke, they should also enclose the pathway to redemption.

Words of Grace seasoned with salt.

This extension of the phrase uses the word salt as a preserving component. Something that is effective when it is spoken, but something that lasts and continues for some time if not forever. Of all the things ever said to us, we can remember only bits and pieces, unless we are reminded. But some things have stuck and are always in our consciousness. When we recall such things, we usually begin by saying, '*I will never forget what was said...*' It was something that has made a lasting impact for good on our lives. It was seasoned with salt.

Out of the heart a man speaks. Matthew 12:34. The more we speak, the more of our heart that is revealed. I pray that when I have spoken to someone, they are better after the encounter than they were before.

Let no corrupt word proceed out of your mouth, but what is good for necessary edification, that it may impart grace to the hearers.

Ephesians 4:29

So then, my beloved brethren, let every man be swift to hear, slow to speak, slow to wrath. James 1:19

Winsome words spoken at just the right time are as appealing as apples gilded in gold surrounded with silver. When you humbly receive wise correction, it adorns your life with beauty and makes you a better person. A reliable, trustworthy messenger refreshes the heart of his master, like a gentle snowfall at harvest time. Clouds that carry no water and a wind that brings no refreshing rain that's what you're like when you boast of a gift that you don't have.
Proverbs 25:11-15 Passion Translation.

A word spoken at the right time in the right way. Or as John Gill [130] puts it, 'a word spoken on its wheels,' that is finely balanced and smoothly proceeds to its destination. The picture of apples in silver is understood by several commentators as a '*golden coloured fruit in a lattice bowl of silver.*' The meaning would be to describe the beauty of appearance and the refreshment such fruit would bring. Such is the effect of the '*winsome words.*' Wise words that bring a correction, and are properly received transform the person to whom they are spoken.

A messenger that delivers the message as it was first spoken, without deviation, interpretation, or addition brings glory to the one who sent him. When we are delivering the Lord's words, his words are good enough, he doesn't need us to embellish them, just repeat them.

The right word is as a cool refreshment in an arduous task. Exaggerations do not bless anyone. They do not encourage or uplift, because they are like clouds that bring no rain, they only disappoint and frustrate.

---

[130] John Gill 1697-1771. A predecessor of Charles Spurgeon.

Grace and Contentment.

My Grace is sufficient for you.
2 Corinthians 12:9.

Let us return to this verse again and speak of the sufficiency of God's Grace. We are people born anew by the Spirit of God in order to inhabit a different place. The Grace of God is preparing us for another world. But at present those heavenly experiences within (2 Corinthians 12:1-6) are buffeted by the reality of the fallen world in which we still live. (2 Corinthians 12: 7-8) As we have said before sometimes the adversary we face is removed, but at other times, as is the case here, it remains. Yet through whatever this affliction is, God's power will still be manifest. The fact that God did mighty things in spite of the affliction, did not minimise the affliction. Our Saviour performed the greatest act of Grace with thorns pressed into his flesh.

His grace is enough to see us through, whatever burden we may be called to carry. The power that flows through us is a contradiction of the weakness in which we serve. But as a result, those that receive Grace know it is not of us, because of ourselves we have nothing to give.

The ignominy of the Cross was God's sign to a sinful world. It still is God's sign to a sinful world. Not in some embellished crucifix on the wall behind the altar, as beautiful as that may be, and meaningful to some, but in the living bodies of God's servants who '*bear in their bodies the marks of the Lord Jesus.*' Were they literal marks, visible to all? Oh yes, they were. 2 Corinthians 11:22-28. They were also marks on the spirit, not visible, (verse 28) as with our Lord, 'now is my soul troubled.' John 12:27.

We are called to be '*Wounded Healers.*' [131]

My Grace is enough.

We should seek the Lord to remove things that we perceive are detrimental to our well-being, health, and ability to serve. However, if those things are not removed then we are to seek the Grace to live with them and the Grace to turn them into instruments that display God's glory. Such Grace produces a contentment.

> *Now godliness with contentment is great gain. For we brought nothing into this world, and it is certain we can carry nothing out.* 1 Timothy 6:6-7.

> *Let your conduct be without covetousness; be content with such things as you have. For He Himself has said, "I will never leave you nor forsake you."* Hebrews 13:5.

> *I know how to be abased, and I know how to abound. Everywhere and in all things, I have learned both to be full and to be hungry, both to abound and to suffer need. I can do all things through Christ who strengthens me.* Philippians 4:12-13.

To live in contentment is to walk in the sufficiency of Grace. Not always striving for things to be different, not blaming someone for the way things are, and not living in regret of one's own actions. But assured that whatever we have to face his Grace is enough.

> *Now, to the one with enough power to prevent you from stumbling into sin and bring you faultless before his glorious presence to stand before him with ecstatic delight, to the only God our Saviour, through our Lord Jesus Christ, be endless glory and majesty, great power and authority—*

---

[131] Sheila Cassidy. Good Friday People.

from before he created time, now, and throughout all the ages of eternity. Amen!
Jude 24-25. Passion Translation

Observed weakness becomes hidden strength. The Lord seems to favour performing his most mighty acts through the most unlikely sources.

But may the God of all grace, who called us to His eternal glory by Christ Jesus, after you have suffered a while, perfect, establish, strengthen, and settle you. 1 Peter 5:10.

Grace and Tolerance.

Growing in Grace. 2 Peter 3:18.

The verse contains a little more, '*and in the knowledge of our Lord Jesus Christ.*' At the moment we receive Christ Jesus as our Saviour and Lord, we stand in the place of Grace. We are justified, accepted and beloved by God. To be a beneficiary of such Grace is an overwhelming thing. '*Now the Grace in which we stand,*' the Grace that is at our right Hand, our left hand, before us and behind us, above us and beneath us must become a part of us.

So often I find that Grace in the believer is understood as tolerance; not having a firm view on anything, respecting everyone's perspective, not judging or criticising someone because they are different, and not correcting things that are wrong. Grace is defined as not being opposed to anything.

This is the doctrine of *Relativism.* There is no objective truth. All truth is relative to the person who believes it and it is no more right or wrong than anyone else's truth. 'Truth' is no different to 'taste,' one person likes chocolate ice-cream, another vanilla.

Against this backdrop we need to look at the life of Jesus, who being full of Grace and Truth, challenged the sinner, denounced the self-righteous, and corrected those in error. With Jesus truth was absolute. He was truth. Of course, Grace 'judges,' in the sense it weighs up the situation. What it doesn't do is 'sentence.' Wisdom demands we weigh up a matter; where it originates, where it leads, and is it authentic.

> *Let us therefore come boldly to the Throne of Grace, that we may obtain mercy and find grace to help in time of need.* Hebrews 4:16.

The term '*The Throne of Grace*' is one of those beautiful oxymorons in scripture where opposites are paired together to reveal truth. The 'Throne' indicates justice, authority and power; Grace, of course, indicates, mercy, forgiveness and understanding. Grace is not '*anything goes,*' but '*anything can be redeemed.*'

We must know in whom we believe. This is '*the knowledge of the Lord.*' We know him by prayer, meditation, worship, and studying the Bible. We take everything we read and hear back to the text itself and see if it is indeed collaborative.

The more we know about Jesus the easier it is to see which expressions of Christianity closely resemble the Jesus that has been revealed to us, and which do not.

The more we know about Jesus the more sensitive our spirit becomes to the presence, or absence, of the Holy Spirit in any given situation. Jesus could say to one person, '*neither do I condemn you, go and sin no more,*' yet to others '*you are children of the devil,*' because he knew who he was.

It is insufficient to leave the meaning of scriptures to the 'scholars'. That is where the medieval church was. Something more is required. Salvation is not in the 'church' it is in Christ, and our personal relationship with him. We have a responsibility to know the scriptures.

We will encounter people who have a different opinion as to what is true and false. Conversely people will view us as having a different opinion to them as to what is true and false. But we must realise that neither our view or theirs is the reference point, it is the scriptures.

The Heart.

What is the sincere motivation of the other person? Are they motivated by a desire to extract themselves and others from the depravity of humanity and journey towards a Christlikeness on the basis of Grace made available through the Cross of Jesus Christ? Then nothing else is more important. If the encounter turns into a relationship, then believe that Christ in you and Christ in them will sort things out. That's Grace.

I remember an incident a few years ago. A church group asked if they could use the church building where I was pastoring for a funeral, because their building would not be big enough for the occasion. I agreed. Now, I knew this group had doctrinal differences to my group. They believed in 'Jesus Only' that God was Jesus and the Father and the Spirit were modes of expression of the same person. We were trinitarian. They believed in 'soul sleep' that is when a person dies their soul sleeps until the resurrection when Jesus returns. We believed in 'absent from the body present with the Lord.' They believed in 'baptismal regeneration' that is, you are only saved by the act of baptism. We believed that baptism followed conversion.

When I was younger, I would have immediately reached for the latest edition of ' *The Kingdom of the Cults* ' and that would have been that. But the Spirit of God seemed to say to me, I want to show you something. I attended the funeral. And guess what? These people loved the Lord Jesus. They sang the same sort of songs. Prayed in the same way. Preached in the same way. The presence of God was in that place the same as he was when we held our services. People committed their lives to Christ at that funeral. And they were extremely grateful for the use of the building.

What am I saying? I think their doctrinal position was insufficient. But God himself didn't seem to consider it such a massive issue. He still blessed them. And so, I reasoned, if this was something that didn't bother the Lord so much, why should it bother me? It never turned into a relationship so we never got to discuss things at a deeper level. But that day I learned a lesson in Grace that has stood me in good stead on other occasions as the years have gone by. What we imagine we know about others is rarely what actually goes on. I grasped a little more of what Jesus meant when he said, '*For he who is not against us is on our side*. Mark 9: 40.

With all respect to God's servant, the late W R Martin, I gave away my copy of the '*Kingdom of the Cults,*' I didn't need it any longer. I decided to treat people who saw things differently as individuals. More than that, individuals who were trying to deal with human depravity just as I was. The scriptures may judge them as incorrect. The people who have taught them are answerable to God for what they have taught, as am I. James 3:1. The people themselves are also responsible for the teachings they have absorbed. 2 Timothy 4:3-4.

> *Receive one who is weak in the faith, but not to disputes over doubtful things. For one believes he may eat all things, but he who is weak eats only vegetables. Let not him who eats despise him who does not eat, and let not him who does not eat judge him who eats; for God has received him. Who are you to judge another's servant? To his own master he stands or falls. Indeed, he will be made to stand, for God is able to make him stand.*

One person esteems one day above another; another esteems every day alike. Let each be fully convinced in his own mind. He who observes the day, observes it to the Lord; and he who does not observe the day, to the Lord he does not observe it. He who eats, eats to the Lord, for he gives God thanks; and he who does not eat, to the Lord he does not eat, and gives God thanks. For none of us lives to himself, and no one dies to himself. For if we live, we live to the Lord; and if we die, we die to the Lord. Therefore, whether we live or die, we are the Lord's. For to this end Christ died and rose and lived again, that He might be Lord of both the dead and the living. But why do you judge your brother? Or why do you show contempt for your brother? For we shall all stand before the judgment seat of Christ. Romans 14:1-10.

Preferences.

As long as the heart of the person is right before God; then whether they express their faith with traditional hymns, contemporary songs, an organ or a band, a cathedral or a hired hall, the service is led by a person in regalia or ordinary clothes, is all a matter of preference. It is not right or wrong. If a particular expression of faith brings someone close to Jesus, then we have nothing to say.

I am fully aware this does not cover every eventuality, but it was part of my journey. It does give an example of how we grow in grace and which can be extrapolated to other situations.

Intolerance.

Grace can be tested to the limit by intolerance. This is usually where Truth and Preference or Truth and Method have merged into one thing. A particular way or method is proclaimed as right and everything else is inferior or wrong.

There is a Pentecostal church not far from where I live, that used to advertise outside its church, *'We only use the King James Version of the Bible here.'* How sad when we have to use the fabric of the scriptures to divide us. If they feel that the first thing their spiritually dying community needs to know, is what version of the Bible they use, I shudder to think what else goes on there.

In such circumstances Grace will bow its head and move on. Grace realises it is a battle not worth fighting. John 2:24. Grace is aware that 'enabling faith' must be present before one can step into Grace.

I understand that we are all trying to deal with the same universal depravity. Some by laws, some by self-righteousness, some by Grace, some by just ignoring it. *'All have sinned'* and all must deal with it. Some have got it right, some nearly right, and others hopelessly wrong. However, when we have to deal with a situation, our ultimate goal is to create a Grace Space where people can at least catch a glimpse of Jesus. We push to one side all the things that are wrong, and the things we think are wrong and to other side all the things that are right, and we think are right, and we walk in the Grace Space, and trust God.

Grace has some inseparable companions.

'Human nature is like a drunk peasant. Lift him into the saddle on one side, over he topples on the other side.'

This is a quote attributed to Martin Luther and has been given several meanings. It will suit us well here. The man on the horse has Grace on one side and regulations on the other. Pick him up from the left he falls to the right; pick him up from the right he falls to the left! Human nature battles to balance Grace. The tendency is always to push to extremes. On the one side we can take Grace to be accommodating of almost anything. On the other side we have so many regulations that there is no longer any Grace. That is why Grace has companions, just to keep us on the horse!

Grace and Truth. John 1:14-17.

Undeserved favour with undiluted revelation. The text is more accurately rendered:

> *The Law came by Moses; Grace and truth came by Jesus Christ.*
> 132

This is not a comparison between Law and Grace, it is how complementary Law and Grace are. The Law was also Truth. It came from God as Jesus had come from God. Jesus did not come to eradicate the Law. Matthew 5:17. He came to fulfil it. The Law revealed God to a lesser extent than Jesus did, but the Law revealed God nevertheless.

The problem had arisen in what had been done with the Law. The same mistake was made as was to be made later by the Christian Bishops. The precise observance of the ritual became redemption in itself. Hebrews chapter 11 makes it abundantly clear, the only way to please God is by Faith. Grace and truth came by Jesus Christ. The Truth is the revelation of God, and Grace is the means whereby we can stand in his presence.

Grace does not water down the awesome holiness of God, neither does it elevate the depravity of mankind. Grace creates a space wherein we can stand in God's Holy presence.

Grace and Peace. Romans 1:7.

Paul begins most of his letters with this greeting. I come to you in peace because I am standing in Grace. The word

---

[132] The majority of translations render the verse without the comparative 'but.'

'peace' on the lips of a '*Hebrew of the Hebrews*,' was the word 'Shalom,' the common Hebrew greeting to this day. Shalom of course is bursting with meaning. It is one of the names of the Messiah, 'Prince of Peace,' Isaiah 9: 6.

I bring you no harm.
I bring you no discomfort.
I bring you no anxiety.
I bring you no conflict.
I bring you things that will lift you up.
I affirm who you are in God.
I wish to strengthen your Faith.
I bring you wholeness, wellness, harmony, and even prosperity. [133]

And because of God's favour towards you, these are not just wishes, they are transferable realities. To approach someone with grace and peace should create an atmosphere of safety and security.

> *For He Himself is our peace, who has made both one, and has broken down the middle wall of separation, having abolished in His flesh the enmity, that is, the law of commandments contained in ordinances, so as to create in Himself one new man from the two, thus making peace.* Ephesians 2:14-15.

Paul is speaking about the hostility between the Jew under the law and the Gentile in trespasses and sin. He has announced and transferred the Shalom to both, and those who have taken his hand have stepped into a new humanity, the Church of Jesus Christ.

We can be generous with Grace because it will never run out. You can pour out Grace every moment of every day, like the

---

[133] John Beeson.

widow's oil, it will never run dry. It is not ours its God's and his resources will never run dry. It is '*Grace on Grace*' unlimited, immeasurable and free. Share the Shalom with whoever you come into contact with.

Grace and Mercy. Titus 1:4.

If '*Grace is the last best word in the English language,*' then Mercy is close on its heels. Grace is the undeserved favour of God. But the consequences of sin can still unfold. Mercy has to do with the consequences of sin and extension of Grace into unfolding events.

> *Out of the depths, O Lord, I cry to You*
> *When I am tempted to despair*
> *Though I might fail to trust Your promises*
> *You never fail to hear my prayer*
> *And if You judged my sin*
> *I'd never stand again*
> *But I see mercy in Your hands.* [134]

Mercy is like the tentacles of Grace reaching into the dark recesses of a sinful world. Mercy operates where the sin of man is unfolding and its consequences of shame, pain and disgrace are gathering momentum. Then suddenly the process is cut short. The chain reaction is broken, and Mercy turns to Grace and says, "Just look who I've found!" And another soul steps into the kingdom.

If you are a legalist, revelling in legislation, Grace and Mercy are your nemesis. They hold justice in an arm lock, they ask righteousness to sit down, and they tell holiness to turn its face away, just for a moment. Then they place the sinner in the hands of the sinless Saviour, and with repentance and confession he stands in the place of Grace and there is no

---

[134] Sovereign Grace Music

condemnation. It is humbling to think that such a powerful force is placed in the hands of believers.

> *Blessed are the merciful for they shall obtain mercy.* Matthew 5:7.

Are we numbered among the 'Merciful.' That is, those who are so affected by the sufferings of others as to be disposed to alleviate them. This is given as evidence of piety, and it is said that they who show mercy to others shall obtain it. [135]

Grace and Calling. Romans 1:5

Paul speaks of receiving 'Grace and apostleship. Paul was called to be an ambassador of Christ to the nations. As such God had placed him in a position to influence the minds of men and establish the framework of the church for all time. Such a position could easily induce pride and prestige. But, like Paul, we are to remember that whatever calling we have it has come from the place of Grace. Whether we have responsibility in a small group, a whole church, or even a group of churches, we are there as a result of undeserved favour. We can serve for a season, or for a lifetime; we can succeed someone or we can be replaced.

It speaks to us of humility;

> *Likewise, you younger people, submit yourselves to your elders. Yes, all of you be submissive to one another, and be clothed with humility, for God resists the proud, but gives grace to the humble.* 1 Peter 5:5.

This is contrary to the philosophies of the world. There to gain favour requires being in the right place at the right time with the right people. It requires being seen and being heard. All

---

[135] Albert Barnes. Notes on the |Bible.

kinds of subterfuge can be employed in order to climb the greasy pole to favour. In addition, favour can be gained by hard work and devotion to duty. As far as the kingdom of God is concerned Undeserved Favour is bestowed on the humble.

Humility is submitting to the sovereign will of God.

> *For thus says the High and Lofty One who inhabits eternity, whose name is Holy, I dwell in the high and holy place; with him who has a contrite heart and humble spirit, to revive the spirit of the heart of the contrite ones.* Isaiah 57:15.

Humility is to acknowledge we are part of the '*all have sinned*' group.

> *For there is not a just man on earth who does good and does not sin.* Ecclesiastes 7:20.

Humility is knowing that we have nothing except what we have received.

> *Now these things, brethren, I have figuratively transferred to myself and Apollos for your sakes, that you may learn in us not to think beyond what is written, that none of you may be puffed up on behalf of one against the other. For who makes you differ from another? And what do you have that you did not receive? Now if you did indeed receive it, why do you boast as if you had not received it?* 1 Corinthians 4:6-7.

These following three definitions of humility correspond to the basic principles of Grace. God is sovereign, all have sinned, and salvation is by Grace alone. We cannot avail ourselves of Grace without humility and we cannot stand firm in Grace unless we walk humbly with God. Micah 6:8. There is no difference between us and the worst of sinners we can imagine, except the Grace of God.

Humility is to accept we will be treated no better than our

Lord.

> *If the world hates you, you know that it hated Me before it hated you. If you were of the world, the world would love its own. Yet because you are not of the world, but I chose you out of the world, therefore the world hates you. Remember the word that I said to you, 'A servant is not greater than his master.' If they persecuted Me, they will also persecute you. If they kept My word, they will keep yours also.* John 15:18-20

Humility is refraining from exercising authority beyond the sphere we have been granted.

> *Yet Michael the archangel, in contending with the devil, when he disputed about the body of Moses, dared not bring against him a reviling accusation, but said, "The Lord rebuke you!" But these speak evil of whatever they do not know; and whatever they know naturally, like brute beasts, in these things they corrupt themselves.* Jude 9-10.

Humility is being comfortable in who we are, not whom we think we are, or would like to be.

> *I, therefore, the prisoner of the Lord, beseech you to walk worthy of the calling with which you were called, with all lowliness and gentleness, with longsuffering, bearing with one another in love, endeavouring to keep the unity of the Spirit in the bond of peace.* Ephesians 4:1-3

Humility is to speak out only on matters with which we have experience or expertise.

> *But reject profane and old wives' fables, and exercise yourself toward godliness.*
> 1 Timothy 4:7.

In these days of the internet this is particularly pertinent. Anyone can pick up any comment and forward it around the world. But where did it come from? Who said it and why and to whom? Is it part of authentic Christian experience? Is it Bible based? If we pass on untested material, we are possible purveyors of false doctrine and are potentially leading people astray. We may feel good about it because we have got a great sounding post, but if it is not Holy Spirit inspired, we are walking in pride.

Grace and Thanksgiving. Colossians 3:17

The final thing that accompanies Grace is thanksgiving. People who stand in Grace are grateful people. Gratitude hammers home the principle we have faced throughout this book, our undeserving status. Thanksgiving lays before us all the benefits of Grace and lays at the feet of Jesus all the honour for obtaining them on our behalf. We '*Enter into his gates with thanksgiving and into his courts with praise.'* (Psalm 100:4) Yet there remains a warning.

> *There is an impulse in the fallen human, in all our hearts to forget that gratitude is a spontaneous response of joy to receiving something. When we forget this, what happens is that gratitude starts to be misused and distorted as an impulse to pay for the very thing that came to us 'gratis' (free). This terrible moment is the birthplace of the 'debtor's ethic.'* [136]

Thanksgiving focuses on what has been achieved in the past, the blessings of the present and the hope for the future. It is never a payment in itself. It is simply bringing honour and glory to our Redeemer and Saviour.

Thanksgiving aligns our hearts to the will of God. 1 Thessalonians 5:18.
Thanksgiving keeps our steps in line with the Lord. Colossians 2:6-7.
Thanksgiving makes the goodness of God known. Isaiah 12:

---

[136] David Mathis.

4-5.
Thanksgiving assures us of safety and stability. Hebrews 12: 28.
Thanksgiving satisfies the longings of the soul. Psalm 107: 8-9.
Thanksgiving guards our hearts and mind. Philippians 4: 4-7.
Thanksgiving opens up to us experiences that defy human understanding. 2 Corinthians 9:15.

We return to the Grace Space; the most beautiful, secure, blessed and privileged place to be. Whatever mounts up out of the depravity of humanity, we can turn and say:

> *As far as the east is from the west, so far has he removed our transgression from us.* Psalm 103: 12.

And however glorious God's holiness shines, we can say;

> *Through the Lord's mercies we are not consumed, because His compassions fail not. They are new every morning; great is Your faithfulness. "The Lord is my portion," says my soul, "Therefore I hope in Him!"* Lamentations 3: 22-24.

> *God of all blessings, source of all life, giver of all grace:*
> *We thank you for the gift of life: for the breath that sustains life,*
> *for the food of this earth that nurtures life, for the love of family and friends*
> *without which there would be no life.*
> *We thank you for the mystery of creation:*
> *for the beauty that the eye can see, for the joy*
> *that the ear may hear, for the unknown*
> *that we cannot behold filling the universe with wonder,*
> *for the expanse of space that draws us beyond the definitions of our selves.*
> *We thank you for setting us in communities:*
> *for families who nurture our becoming,*
> *for friends who love us by choice,*
> *for companions at work, who share our burdens and daily tasks,*

for strangers who welcome us into their midst,
for people from other lands who call us to grow in understanding,
for children who lighten our moments with delight,
for the unborn, who offer us hope for the future.
We thank you for this day: for life and one more day to love,
for opportunity and one more day to work for justice and peace,
for neighbours and one more person to love and by whom be
loved, for your grace and one more experience of your presence,
for your promise: to be with us, to be our God, and to give
salvation.

For these, and all blessings, we give you thanks, eternal, loving
God,
through Jesus Christ we pray. Amen. [137]

The Grace of the Lord Jesus be with you all. Amen.
Revelation 22:21

---

[137] *Vienna Cobb Anderson*

The Grace Space

Bibliography.

The Bible used in this book is the New King James version

Title	publisher	author
The Bible NKJV	Broadman and Holman	
The Bible NIV	Zondervan	
The Passion Translation.	Broadstreet	B Simmons
The Interlinear Greek-English New Testament.	Bagster	A Marshall
Vicars of Christ.	Corgi	P de Rosa
The Atonement.	Bethany Fellowhip	A Barnes
From Christ to Constantine.	IVP	M A Smith
Documents of the Christian church	OUP	H Bettenson
The Bible Speaks Today	IVP	editor J Stott.
Through Many Dangers.	Evangelical Press	B H Edwards
The Unfailing Stream.	Sovereign World	D Allen
Church History	Pickering and Inglis	A Miller
All the Doctrines of the Bible.	Pickering and Inglis	H Lockyer

Dialogue with Trypho the Jew	online	A L Williams
Institutes Of the Christian Religion	online	J Calvin
Augustine the City of God	online	
Exploring Manichaeism	online	K Samples
Martin Luther Commentaries	godrules.net	
Enchiridion	online	Augustine
Biography of Arminius	online	Brittanica
Summa Theologica	online	T Acquinas
Commentary on Romans	online	M Luther
What's so Amazing about Grace	Zondervan	P Yancey
Elect in the Son	Bethany House	R Shank
Life in the Son	Bethany House	R Shank
Floodgates	Whitaker House	D Parsons
Commentaries J F B	Oliphants	JFB
Clarke	Baker	A Clarke
Barnes notes on the Bible Origen	Kregel online	A Barnes
Open Theism	online	
Dictionary of NT Theology	Paternoster	ed. C Brown

Other books by the same author

Reasons to Believe.
A Commentary on the Gospel of John.   **Amazon**
This book provides a commentary on John's gospel which is structured around the series of 'sevens' in the text. As such it shines fresh light on the ancient text and presents a highly readable devotional source. It emphasises John's own declared intention, 'these things are written so that you may believe.'

The Kingdom Unveiled.
A study on the Kingdom of God.   **Amazon**
This book deals with many of the difficult matters that are associated with the concept of the kingdom of God. Such as the origin of the concept; the purpose and meaning of parables; the nature of Satan and evil; the kingdom and the church; the kingdom and the nation of Israel; the kingdom and our understanding of the end of this age; spiritual warfare; and how the kingdom shapes our lives in such matters of being peacemakers, stewards, and priests in our communities.

THE AUTHOR

Graham Field is a retired Pentecostal minister living in the
UK. He is married to Ann and has two grown children,
Sharon and David.
He has planted and pastored Churches in South Africa and
the UK.
He has been a lecturer in Biblical Archaeology and Hebraic
Studies at the International Bible Training College, Burgess
Hill, West Sussex, UK.
He has served on the Board of the International Christian
Embassy, Jerusalem.
He holds a Diploma from the Theological College of Southern
Africa and a Degree from International Correspondence
University USA.

The Grace Space